Lord,
The People Have Driven Me On

Lord,
The People Have Driven Me On

[handwritten inscription: To: Deonis C. Dickinson Success to you in your study of my friend – Whitney Young. July 27, 1982 Benjamin Mays]

by Benjamin E. Mays

VANTAGE PRESS
New York / Washington / Atlanta
Los Angeles / Chicago

Excerpts from *Born to Rebel* by Dr. Benjamin E. Mays, copyrighted
1972, used with permission of Charles Scribner's Sons.

Dedicated to the elementary and secondary school students enrolled in the public schools of Atlanta, Georgia, and to those students enrolled in the public schools of the nation, and to Morehouse men everywhere.

Foreword

Benjamin Elijah Mays, the mentor of Martin Luther King, Jr., and a host of Morehouse College students, has had a magnificent career as a teacher, preacher, college president, and public officer. His life is a legend of fostering unity out of contradictions. As a Pullman porter and professor, he demonstrated that honest work is honorable. A teacher of theology and mathematics, he united religion and science. As president of a college and of a public school board, he correlated elementary, secondary, and higher education and integrated black, brown, and white populations. He transformed that which should be changed, transcended that which could not, and endured difficulties that were beyond his control. A moral man with a great mind, he has used it for the advancement of the people.

Charles Vert Willie
Harvard University

I am indebted to Doctor Jeannette Hume Lutton, Dr. Addie Mitchell, Prof. Cordelia Blount, and Lerone Bennett, Senior Editor of *Ebony* magazine.

B.E.M.

Lord,
The People Have Driven Me On

Chapter One

Beginning with my mother, my oldest sister, and my other brothers and sisters who were sympathetic with my desire to learn and get an education, I have felt my indebtedness to people. Mother never went to school a day in her life, but she prayed that God would help me in my ambition to go to school. Susie, my oldest sister, a good fourth-grade scholar, taught me to say the alphabet, to read, and to count. When I went to school at the age of six, I started off amazing the teacher. The members of my family were proud of my learning ability and never expected me to use incorrect English, although I heard it in our home. I always felt that I had to do well for the family's sake. Although the members of my family had not distinguished themselves in any art, profession, trade, or technology, and had accumulated no wealth, I was as proud of my family as if they had achieved some degree of fame or greatness.

Even my father was willing for me to attend the one-room schoolhouse where classes ran four months a year, as long as I was satisfied to come home to the farm, on the first of March, and go back to school when all the cotton had been picked by October 31. Though poor, the family was fairly close-knit.

The closeness was due, in part, to the religious nature of our family. Every evening, and some mornings, mother called us around the fireside, and we got down on our knees and prayed, with mother giving the lead prayer. We children often prayed also, and, as a rule,

1

father joined us if he had not already gone to bed. These experiences made a tremendous impression on me, and I remember them as if they were yesterday.

At the one-room school, students respected me because I knew more than they did, and the teacher thought I was something special. She often "bragged on" me, and I liked it. In fact, I fell in love with my teacher; therefore, I had to continue to do well, because she was my teacher and my first love.

On the second Sunday in November (church convened only one Sunday a month), my teacher told my parents, with a crowd listening, "Bennie is smart." This stimulated me, and I felt obligated to live up to her expectations. On the second Sunday in June of each year, we had Children's Day. The pastor did not preach that Sunday, but instead he urged all the young people to learn a piece to recite on that day.

This assignment was grist for my mill! I was eager to recite. I was eight years old and had chosen and committed to memory the fifth chapter of Matthew for the next Children's Day. When I finished speaking, the people went wild. Old women waved their handkerchiefs; old men stamped their feet, and the audience stood up, including the young, and applauded me lustily, loud, and long. How could I let this crowd down? They said that I would do something worthwhile in the world, that I would be a Booker Washington or a Fred Douglass. The pastor, Rev. James F. Marshall, predicted that I would preach, and I was a "marked" boy from that day forward. Though preaching was one Sunday a month, there was Sunday school every Sunday. There was no graded lesson, but I walked four miles—eight miles round trip—sitting with my elders, commenting on the lesson, asking questions. I was an unusual boy to them, and they told me I would someday be somebody; this praise encouraged me. They thought that if any youngster walked eight miles round trip to Sunday school and seven miles round trip to the one-room brick-house school, he must have a purpose or be possessed with a dream. All of those people are dead now, but I still feel that I cannot let them down, for they are some of the witnesses who have driven me on.

All of this is a part of my experience: being a field hand, pulling fodder, chopping cotton, scattering guano, and plowing a mule. How well do I remember plowing my mule to the end of the row, hitching him to a tree, and going down in the woods to pray, asking God to help me to get an education, and to move out of my way every impediment that kept me from accomplishing this goal. I prayed the same prayer at night. In the moonlight, with the heavens bedecked with stars and planets, I stole away from the house and prayed in the moonlight. It was always the same prayer, asking God to take away the impediment that blocked the path that led to an education for me. It was the wrong prayer perhaps, because the impediment that stood in my way was my father; however, God helped me to get an education without taking my father. For that, I thank God.

My family was poor but proud. The members of my family never accepted as right the segregation and degradation that covered the South "as the dew covers Dixie." This was true of the members of the Mount Zion Church, as a whole. They were noted for their pride. Some few of them owned their land, but most of them were renters, sharecroppers, and wage hands. Many of the single young men of the church owned their own horses and buggies. It was interesting to note these young men coming to church late in order to be seen, and also to serve notice that they would carry their girl friends home. My brother John was one of them. He had a white mule and a white rubber-tire buggy. Johnnie was the "sporty" one in my family.

These experiences remind me that one does not have to be a slave, though his environment treats him as one, and is designed.to make him accept slavery as a fact. My father demonstrated this very well. In my county, Greenwood, a black man was not supposed to pass white people and throw dust or mud on them, however slow they were driving. My father would often, if in a hurry, drive up beside the white man who was driving too slowly and say, "Excuse me, boss, I am in a hurry." I knew my father was not servile, for if I heard it once, I heard my father tell hundreds of times how he beat two white men, knocking down one while the other one was getting up. Thinking of the heroic deeds of my father and of those captives who fought and died on board ship, rather than be slaves in America, how can I forsake them? They, too, are among the people who have driven me on.

The teachers in my life have played a significant role in making me what I am today. From my grade-school teachers at McCormick, South Carolina, on to State College in Orangeburg, South Carolina, to those at Virginia Union University in Richmond, Virginia, to my instructors at Bates College in Lewiston, Maine, and to those professors at the University of Chicago—all of these individuals have had a tremendous impact on my life. Even those who never taught me in their classes put their imprint upon me, as their scholarly presence pervaded the learning environment in which I found myself. Most of these mentors are dead, but I feel obligated to pay my debts to them. The further I went up the educational ladder, the more I could understand my ability to learn. These teachers opened up new vistas of learning and inspired me to do things that I never thought I could accomplish. It might be illuminating to the reader if I name a few of these dedicated souls.

I went to McCormick at the age of fifteen. There

were only two teachers at the school, Reverend J. H. Walker and his wife. They taught all of the subjects that were offered. Observing my aptness, Reverend Walker used me as "Exhibit A," calling on me to recite when other students failed. In the school forum, I was often called upon to speak, and sometimes I presided. Mrs. J. H. Walker was an attractive woman, always well-groomed. Reverend Walker was pastor of a church in Bamberg, South Carolina. Mrs. Walker often sent me to the train to meet her husband and to carry his bags to the school, about a quarter of a mile from the station. Reverend Walker had little money; therefore, he had to make more money than the school could pay him, in order to support his wife and two daughters. The McCormick School was an association school, of which the Reverend Marshall, our pastor at Mount Zion Baptist church, was the moving spirit that kept it going. In those days of limited schools for Negroes, or no schools at all, association schools sprang up all over the South for the training of black students. Reverend Walker got around in McCormick on a bicycle. He was an impressive man, who, along with his wife, definitely left his mark on me.

I soon learned that the McCormick School was not much better than my brick-house school in Greenwood County—the same old story: four months in school and back to the farm for eight months. When I told Reverend Walker and Reverend Marshall that I would not be back, they were sorry. Reverend Walker knew that State College was a better place than McCormick, and urged me to go there. Reverend Marshall was sorry to have me leave McCormick, and in response to my letter informing him that I would not return, he wrote: "I planned to make you a student assistant to Reverend Walker." It was clear then that with or without the consent of my elders, I had to take my life in my own hands. Sink or swim, I had to pursue my own course in

5

search of an education. McCormick was good for me. I learned there that I could not let students—neither boys nor girls who had no thought of learning—divert me from my course. In 1909, when I went to McCormick, it was a great day. I boarded the train for McCormick, only twenty-four miles from Greenwood. From that day to this one, I have admired trains and think that it is unfortunate that high-speed modern air travel has caused passenger trains to become virtually nonexistent. It seems to me that there should be one train a day connecting the major cities of this country.

When there was nothing more for me at the brick-house school, and the McCormick school had only a little more to offer, I wanted to go to Benedict College in Columbia, South Carolina, or to State College in Orangeburg. Once more, the battle with father had to be fought! Nevertheless, I wrote to Benedict and to the State College high school departments. I finally chose State College because it was less expensive. I could go there for six dollars a month, and the fare from Ninety-Six, the nearest train stop to Orangeburg, was only $3.05. I knew that I could earn this much, even if father sent me nothing. When Father saw that I was determined to go to a better school and realized that I had to have money in order to do so, he angrily threw a ten-dollar bill at me. I made my way to Orangeburg without Father's blessing, but with my mother's prayers. On my arrival, Miss Julia Mae Williams, teacher of the seventh grade, gave me an examination and then took me to Professor N. C. Nix, telling him that I belonged in the eighth grade.

According to custom, for the first two years at State College, I was called home at the end of February in order to work on the farm. I was vividly aware that time has swift wings. I was nineteen, and not once in my life had I been able to remain in school more than four months in any year. In my third year, after my four months' stay at State College, when my father

6

again sent for me to come home to work on the farm, I was determined that, at whatever cost, I would remain at State for the full term. I invoked the help of Professor Nix, my high school mathematics teacher, who wrote to my father asking him to let me finish the school year. Father was adamant. I wrote to Father, explaining that I could never get anywhere if I continued to go to school only four months a year. I told him, too, that I would not come home until school closed in May. At this point, the break with my father came, and it was final; for I disobeyed him without regret and with no pangs of conscience. It was now crystal clear to me that I had taken my education into my own hands, and that I could not and must not permit even my father to dictate or to determine my future. Father threatened to send the sheriff for me, but fortunately he did not carry out his threat. Had he done so, I would have been compelled to go home.

Six dollars a month is not much money, but it was a great deal for a boy who had none, who indeed had nothing but a consuming desire to be somebody worthwhile. My brother John, who had a farm of his own, promised to send me three dollars a month for the next two years. The other three dollars I would have to earn, plus a little extra money for laundry and incidentals. Professor Jones, who was called "Big Time" by the students, gave me a job. It was not a pleasant one. It was cleaning outhouses at midnight, after everyone else had gone to bed. There was no indoor plumbing in the dormitories in those days. This was nauseating work, but it paid six dollars a month. With what my brother sent me, and what I earned, I could pay my expenses and I could stay in school for the full term.

At this time, I was on my own; never again would I have to depend on my father; my future was in my hands. Luckily for me, the Pullman Company was coming South each spring to recruit students for summer jobs. If a student was tall enough, strong enough, and

7

had seventeen dollars to buy his cap and uniform, he had work for the summer. The Pullman Company paid the fare to New York and deducted it from the first money the student earned. I jumped at the opportunity to earn my way and to go North for the first time. Orangeburg, 125 miles from home, was the farthest I had ever traveled.

How was I to get seventeen dollars? Since I was the ranking student in my class, once more "Exhibit A" when visitors came, I thought it would be easy to borrow seventeen dollars. Not so! It was necessary for me to approach five teachers before I found one who was willing to lend me seventeen dollars. This experience, and one which I had in Chicago some years later, made me vow that once I got a job and held it, I would never again be without money. This is a vow which, since 1921, I have never broken, nor even bent!

I have always been grateful to Professor Bollie Levister who, without hesitation, said that he would be glad to let me have the money. He told me that he was making the loan to me without requiring me to sign a note, but advised that if ever I had any money to lend, to be sure that the borrower signed a note. The realization that Professor Levister trusted me was as great a lift to my spirit as his money was to my practical need. I was proud and happy, when I got my first paycheck, to send a seventeen-dollar money order to Professor Levister. Several years ago, I met his two daughters, who were small girls on the campus when I was at State. I told them of their father's gracious generosity to me and assured them that if ever I could do anything for them, it would be my pleasure to do so. When my book, *Disturbed About Man*, was published in April 1969, I was happy to send one of Professor Levister's daughters an autographed copy, expressing appreciation for what her father had done for me. Recently, I sent the other daughter a copy of *Born to Rebel*.

Chapter Two

I spent the summer of 1915, and several more summers, as a Pullman porter, working out of Grand Central Station in New York, and South Station in Boston. I did fairly well. Indeed, I felt that I had done extremely well, for I was able to return to school in the fall of 1915 all dressed up. I had two suits. Never before had I owned two good suits—or even one good suit! I knew for the first time the thrill that comes to a boy who earns his own money and spends it as he chooses.

New York was a bit disappointing to me. I had heard so much about it, but it never quite came up to my expectation, not even to this day. Then, too, I found unexpected prejudice in the North. It was not the depressing, terrifying kind that I knew in South Carolina, but in some situations, I found that it was just as ego-wounding and just as humiliating. There were restaurants that would not serve Negroes and hotels where Negroes could not stay. In Detroit, one hot day, I went into a place to buy a cool drink. The attendant sold the "soda water" to me, but smashed the glass, from which I drank the soda, onto the floor—shattering it in a hundred pieces, as soon as I placed it on the counter. There was no doubt about his feeling toward Negroes.

For graduation, the high school at State College required the completion of thirteen grades. Having entered State in the eighth-grade class, I expected to stay in the grades and the high school for six years. Much to my delight, however, I finished in five years, completing the last four years' work in only three years. Professor Nix sometimes left me in charge of the class. One day, when I told a classmate that he had not worked a problem correctly, he flew into a rage and pulled his knife on me, and a friend from his hometown came forth to help him "do me in." The fight did not actually develop, but when I related the incident to Professor Nix, he said, "Mays, you can do the work in the next class. I am promoting you now to that class. It is nothing but jealousy, and I am taking you out of there." The next day, I went into the junior class, and I was graduated from high school in 1916, as valedictorian. In the sixteen years since I had entered the first grade at the age of six, I had spent only seventy-three months in school—the equivalent of eight nine-month terms of schooling. Had I been able to complete each school year, without being taken out for farm work, I would have been graduated at fourteen years of age instead of at twenty-one. I regret those "lost years."

Although the high-school teachers at State were excellent, I am well aware that there are gaps in my education that I have never been able to close. Despite the fact that the later years brought me membership in Phi Beta Kappa, the Ph.D. from a great university, and honorary doctorates from forty-seven distinguished colleges and universities, the lost years and the accompanying deficits took their toll. There are many things that one must learn and read in elementary and high school if he is to have a good foundation; otherwise, it is too late, for each passing day makes its own new demands. If one had time to catch up on the reading that he missed as a child, the end result would be different. I am sure that I would have read many books in my childhood, had they been available. They were not in the brick-house school, not in my home, not in the community. No library was available to me.

I studied hard and long in high school, not because I had to in order to keep up with my classmates, but because I really wanted to learn. I was aiming for something; I did not know what. Vaguely, yet ardently, I longed to know, for I sensed that knowledge could set me free. The vast majority of the students at State in my day did not really apply themselves; few students appeared to have the desire to learn. The boys seemed to have their minds on the girls; the girls seemed to have their minds on the boys. The boys would sit on campus, looking at their girl friends for hours at a time and for hours at a time, the girls would parade the campus, to be seen by the boys. Study or no study, however, most of them passed their work. The few students who did apply themselves to study were considered oddballs or called bookworms. I was one who was deemed to be both an oddball and a bookworm.

I can recall the names of almost all the students who did serious work. The serious-minded, purposeful students, rather than the "don't care" boys, were my friends.

It did my soul good in 1911, to find at State College an all-Negro faculty and a Negro president. There were good teachers, holding degrees from Benedict College, Biddle University (now Johnson C. Smith), Lincoln University in Pennsylvania, Fisk University, and other colleges. President Robert Shaw Wilkinson was a graduate of Oberlin; he was handsome and walked erect and with assurance. His wife, Marian Birnie Wilkinson, was one of the finest women I have ever known. She fought racial injustice and discrimination, and the white merchants who sold to the school paid her the unusual tribute of calling her "Mrs." Wilkinson. She had a proud carriage, and I enjoyed seeing her walk across campus. The inspiration that I received at State College was, and is today, of incalculable value.

All of my teachers lavished praise and encouragement on me because I studied hard and made good grades. Perhaps the one who inspired me most was Profesor Nelson C. Nix. He had an interesting way of challenging the students who wanted to be challenged. When virtually the whole class was stuck on a problem in mathematics, Nix would say, "You boys can't work these problems? The white boys at the University of South Carolina are eating these problems up!" All of the forces in my environment had been designed to make me accept the notion that the quality of my mind was different from that of white boys; but Nix challenged us with his talk about the white boys at the University of South Carolina once too often for me. He said it one day just after he had returned a test paper to me marked "100." After class, I asked Professor Nix how much more than 100 percent would the white boys at the University of South Carolina make on the test. He patted me on the back saying, "Ah, my boy, they wouldn't beat *you*!" This did not quite reassure me. The very fact that Nix kept referring to white boys made me wonder sometimes if he, himself, did not believe that there was a difference in the mentality of black and white students.

Professor Nix had an A.B. and, I believe, a degree in theology from Benedict College. He had not earned the master's degree in mathematics, but he knew mathematics and he was a good teacher. He had studied at least one summer at the University of Chicago; but, from the proud and proprietary way he talked about the university, one might have thought that he had earned the Ph.D. there. It was he who made me want to attend the University of Chicago some day. One summer, while still a student at State College and working out of Grand Central Station in New York as a Pullman porter, I was delighted to be assigned to a car bound for Chicago. While there, I took the streetcar and rode to the South Side of the city to see the University of Chicago. I was impressed. I wrote a card to a classmate, Mattie Mae Fitzgerald, telling her that some day I would be a student at the University of Chicago. This prophecy came true on January 3, 1921, when I enrolled there. Let me review now other teachers at South Carolina State who have driven me on. E. A. Lawrence was a teacher of civics at State College. He was an attractive, well-dressed man. He would always call on me when the other students in the class could not answer the question. When I was asked a question, I prefaced my response by saying, "In addition to what has been said, my answer is—." This made a deep impression on him. Lawrence took a few moments to tell the other students how thoroughly I did my work. He often told me that I would do well in life.

There were teachers at State who did not teach me in academic courses, but were, nevertheless, instructors whom I admired: Waterman in tailoring, Davis in painting, Lewis in harness-making and shoe-repairing, and Pierce in carpentry. At State, one day every week was given to trades, and I took my share of trade courses, though I was evidently designed for an academic career. I started out under Profesor Lewis, instructor in shoe-repairing and harness-making, but I found I had no aptitude for Instructor Lewis's craft. Later, I went to Instructor Waterman, but I had no aptitude for tailoring, either. I went next to painting with Mr. Davis. I liked painting, and Davis and I hit it off very well.

I was known throughout the college, and I left State feeling that all eyes at State College were watching me, expecting me to hold up the banner of S.C.C. Among those who helped me there, I have already mentioned Professor Jones, who had charge of buildings and grounds. As stated previously, he paid me six dollars a month to pick up paper and go with him at midnight to clean the out-of-doors toilets—dirty work to be sure, but honorable work that enabled me to get an education. I also remember Miss Kanty, who made Paul Lawrence Dunbar become alive to me; H. P. Butler, who made me appreciate Latin and Shakespeare; and Reverend P. P. Watson, who preached the Christian religion with great effectiveness.

There were others at State who encouraged me on my way. One was B. F. Hubert, professor of Agriculture. He was a graduate of Massachusetts Agriculture College, located at Amherst, Massachusetts. Hubert came from that family of Huberts around Sparta, Georgia. Seeing Hubert walking across the campus, with head high, body erect, shoulders thrown back, one thought that he owned the campus. There were many Hubert boys and girls, and I believe they all graduated from Morehouse or Spelman. F. Marcelius Staley was another who encouraged me. After being disillusioned when I did not go straight to Dartmouth or Brown, Staley advised me to go to Virginia Union. I accepted his advice and entered the freshman class at Virginia Union, in September 1916. I thought of Brown because John Hope went there, and I had met him when I was a student at South Carolina State. I thought of Dartmouth because it was Daniel Webster's school. Two things frightened me away from Dartmouth and Brown, cost and curriculum. I had no money, and the curriculum "scared" me. All of the foreign languages seem to have been taught at these two universities, as well as chemistry, physics, and biology—courses that I did not know existed. I thought I couldn't make it there academically.

I was amused, when I got to Richmond, to find that many Virginians considered themselves "Northerners," and some of them referred to me as "my friend Mays, from the South!" From the four-month country school to Virginia Union. I found a more serious-minded student body at Virginia Union in Richmond than I had previously known. The college course was firmly established there, although, like other colleges for Negroes, Virginia Union had its academy or high-school department. There were a few seniors in the college, and one or two in the seminary, who could be respected for their scholarship and character. There were a few students, too, in my class whom I admired and who were worthy competitors in the pursuit of academic excellence. I got the impression that the faculty at Union was able. It was a racially-mixed faculty and, for the first time in my life, I came to know a few white persons who expressed an interest in Negroes. This was a wholly new experience for me. The one thing that impressed me most at Virginia Union was the fact that, in the opinion of all of us students, the Negro professors were just as able as the white ones. The Negro teachers presented a good image to the Negro students, an image that was perhaps quite as important as the content of their courses.

I did well academically at Virginia Union. I took college mathematics, English, German, and Latin. At the end of the first semester of my freshman year, approximately half of my classmates had flunked college algebra, and I was chosen to teach mathematics to those who had failed. The money for teaching the course came as a boon, for I had not saved enough money as a Pullman porter the previous summer to carry me through the year. A dining-hall job and the student-teaching job enabled me to pay my bills for the year.

Despite the claim that Virginians were Northerners, I found the same racial pattern in Richmond that I had experienced in South Carolina. Orangeburg and Greenwood did not have streetcars. We walked where we wanted to go. Richmond had its segregated streetcars, with Negroes sitting in the rear. I was seeing segregation in a large Southern city for the first time, but it was the same old segregation that I had known since infancy. We freshmen had heated arguments about whether Negroes should or should not patronize the segregated theaters in Richmond. I went to a segregated theater just once during my school year at Virginia Union, and I decided then, in the academic year 1916–17, that never again would I go to a segregated theater. I have kept that vow. I held then, as I do now, that there is a difference between voluntary segregation and compulsory segregation. One has to accept compulsory segregation or pay a penalty, but one does not have to accept voluntary segregation. I had to accept Richmond's segregation on the streetcars if I wanted to get where I had to go. But it was in no way necessary for me to volunteer to accept an embarrassing seat in a Jim Crow theater. Another situation that we students at Union discussed was the fact that all of the Negro schools in Richmond had white principals. We could discuss this, but we couldn't do anything to bring about a change. Richmond Negroes generally did not even discuss it very much. They accepted what "had always been."

Before leaving Virginia Union, I had an important decision to make. I was old enough to be a soldier in World War I. In November 1916, Woodrow Wilson had been reelected president of the United States, partly on the slogan, "He kept us out of war." But despite Wilson's intentions, on April 6, 1917, the United States entered the war against Germany. I can still hear the silence of that Richmond audience when William Howard Taft spoke there, ending his speech with the statement, "The United States is now at war with Germany."

A Jim Crow officers' training camp was set up in Des Moines, Iowa, and college Negroes were being recruited to go to Des Moines to be trained to become officers in the United State Army. Wilson coined a phrase that became famous: "We are fighting to make the world safe for democracy." Many of my friends were making applications for a place at the camp in Des Moines. What was I to do? I had known everything but democracy in South Carolina. I was finishing my freshman year in college and would be twenty-three my next birthday—easily five years behind, owing to the crippling educational circumstances imposed upon me by my native state of South Carolina. I registered for military service, but did not volunteer to go to Des Moines.

Chapter Three

I decided to go on to Bates College and wait to be drafted. I did not seek induction, nor did I join the R.O.T.C. at Bates, as President George Colby Chase advised. When the draft forms came, one question on them was, "Do you claim exemption for any reason?" I replied, "No, except that I am a student for the ministry." I was classified 4-D, and the war ended before I was reclassified. If I had been visibly present in Greenwood County, I might not have been deferred. I might even have been killed.

I enjoyed my year at Virginia Union and left only because I was still determined to go to a New England college. My mathematics teacher, Roland A. Wingfield, and Charles E. Hadley, the Y.M.C.A. faculty adviser who also taught chemistry, were both graduates of Bates. Learning of my desire to study in New England, they wrote to President Chase of Bates in my behalf. As a result, I was accepted as a sophomore on probation, with the understanding that if I did passing work in the first six weeks' tests, I would be a full-fledged sophomore. I passed my tests successfully. I had developed a determination that nothing could stop me, except ill health or death.

I wanted to go to New England primarily for one reason: my total southern environment proclaimed that Negroes were inferior people, and that indictment included me. I needed to prove this widespread feeling to be a false one. The manner in which white people treated Negroes, the difference in school buildings and in the length of time of the school term, the difference in salaries paid Negro and white teachers, the inability of Negroes to vote, the brutal treatment of Negroes (including lynching), said to me that whites viewed Negroes as nobodies. One particular experience I had in South Carolina said this most loudly of all. A white physician in the Epworth community slapped me temporarily blind at the post office, as I was waiting to get the family mail. He said, "Get out of the way, you black rascal; you are trying to look too good anyway." In his eyes, I had committed three unpardonable sins: I had been born black; I kept myself clean; and I stood erect. The physician considered the latter forms of behavior unbecoming in Negroes. They were supposed to approach white people with body bowed, cringing and kowtowing. Why didn't I strike back? I was afraid to do so. The store was filled with white people in overalls, smoking and chewing tobacco. If I had attempted to defend myself, I would have been shot down and killed like a rabbit. The white man was law, court and jury. The economic dependence of Negroes upon whites, the way in which news about Negroes was handled in the press, and, most of all, the manner in which Negroes accepted their denigration tended to make each new generation believe that it was, indeed, inferior.

Although I had never accepted my assigned status—or lack of it—I knew that I had to prove my worth and ability. How could I know that I was not inferior to the white man, having never had a chance to compete with him? Since such competition was impossible in the South, the arena had to be elsewhere. I had to get out of Greenwood County. I had the notion (fallacious, of course) that the Yankee by nature was intellectually superior to the Southern white man, and that if I could compete in New England with the naturally superior Yankee, I would have *prima facie* evidence that Negroes were not inferior. It did not take me long to discover that Yankee superiority was as mythical as Negro inferiority. In my early years, however, the conviction was strong and the challenge very real. Yankee superiority was the gauntlet thrown down; I had to pick it up.

President Hovey of Virginia Union did not take kindly to my going to Bates. The friends with whom I worked out of Grand Central Station as a summer Pullman porter were even more insistent that I remain in Richmond. Their argument was that I would freeze to death in Maine, and that Maine was too far away from South Carolina in case I had to go home in an emergency. I was grateful for the interest in my welfare that prompted their advice, but once more, I had to make my own decision. I entered Bates in September 1917.

My friends were almost prophetic in their prediction about my freezing in Maine. Since I was too far away to go home at Christmastime, I stayed on the campus through the 1917 holidays. On Christmas Day, it was forty–four below zero—one of the coldest Christmases in Lewiston's history, and my first winter out of the South. I remember well that it was a clear day. The Maine sky was beautiful, and the ground sparkled with snow. I accepted the job of clearing away the snow at President Chase's residence. I had not been working very long when the president's daughter invited me to come inside and get warm. I assured her that I was quite comfortable, not knowing that I had reached the point of numbness where I could not recognize how cold I was. When I finally did go inside, my fingers, toes, and ears were aching most painfully. I was told that had I remained out in the cold much longer, my toes and fingers would probably have had to be amputated. For several months thereafter, my toes felt numb. Even now, more than fifty years later, my feet are still very sensitive to cold. I wear two pairs of socks in winters; and when I am sitting indoors, I can tell when the temperature is dropping outside. My feet are my thermometer. I say jokingly that my feet got cold in Maine in 1917, and they have never been warm since!

The weather was cold, but the hearts at Bates were warm. It was a dreary day and a lonely ride from New York to Lewiston, Maine, that day in September, 1917. I was traveling to a strange land where I didn't know a single soul. The Bates brand of friendliness started on the train. As I recall, I was the only Negro aboard. A Bates student, returning to school, introduced himself and asked where I was going. When I answered, "Bates College," he told me that he was a student there and would be glad to help me find housing. This he did, and I have never forgotten, nor can I ever forget, his warm friendliness. Shortly after arriving in Lewiston, I met Julian Coleman, a Negro in the senior class, from Pawtucket, Rhode Island. That first night when he offered me shelter marked the beginning of a close friendship that lasted until his death a few years ago. He was one of the finest men I have ever known.

There were only a few other Negroes at Bates during my first years there. I was living in a predominantly white world, and how different a world it was from any I had known before! The teachers and students were friendly and kind. I was treated as a person, as a human being, respected for what I was. Faculty and students, men and women, greeted me when I met them on campus and on the street. We met and mingled as peers, not as "superior" versus "inferior." This was a new experience for me. I was getting another view of white men, a radically different view. They were not all my enemies. For the first time, whether on campus or in the town of Lewiston, whether alone or in a group, I felt at home in the universe.

I do not mean to give the impression that there was no racial prejudice at Bates in my time. We Negro students quickly spotted and knew the students who gave evidence of prejudice, but their number was negligible and did not exercise any significant influence on the Bates College family as a whole or on the Negro students in particular. When on one occasion, I was called "nigger" by a white student waiter, the white students handled the situation so decisively that there was no need for me to speak. On three other occasions when I fancied there was discrimination, I think now that I was mistaken. There were only a few Negroes in the whole state of Maine; and in the small towns and rural areas, a Negro was really a novelty. White children stared at me, their eyes wide with curiosity, but there was nothing mean, nothing offensive in their curiosity. To the great embarrassment of a friend, his small daughter once tried to rub off my dark skin and asked me why I didn't have skin like her daddy's. Once in Lewiston, a small white boy saw me and called to his mother, "Here is a nigger!" Such incidents were rare, and there really was very little manifestation of racial prejudice in Maine.

When I arrived at Bates, I had ninety dollars in my pocket. A year's expenses totaled about $600. Without Bates's concern for me, I would never have been able to meet my financial obligations there for my three years. Bates had a rule not to give scholarships to transfer students, not even to one with a "straight A" record, such as I had brought with me from Virginia Union. For the first year, I was able to borrow some money from the college's loan fund. In my junior and senior years, I was on scholarship. I worked in the dining hall for a while, was a student helper in the library, served as janitor of a small academic building, washed dishes in a restaurant in downtown Lewiston, worked as a Pullman porter during summers and holidays, and painted floats one summer in a shipyard in

Boston. My brother, who was farming in South Carolina, sent me fifty dollars while I was at Bates, and a friend in South Carolina sent five or ten dollars monthly. Obviously, I did not suffer from affluence of any kind.

I had read in the Bates catalog that very soon after the opening of the school year, the sophomore declamation contest would be held. I had won two prizes in public speaking during my high-school years at State. I didn't know whether or not one could choose his own declamation subject, but I decided to take a chance. I had been greatly impressed with an oration entitled "The Supposed Speech of John Adams." I committed it to memory, and all summer long I rehearsed it before the mirror of a Pullman car on the New York Central Railroad. When the announcement of the sophomore declamation contest was made, I presented myself, asking permission to use the speech that I already knew quite well. I was permitted to enter and was chosen as one of the nine students to compete in the finals.

Someone had told me that Mrs. Fred Pomeroy, wife of Professor Pomeroy, who was head of the Biology Department, was good in speech and drama, having studied speech in Boston. I was taking a course in biology and asked Professor Pomeroy to find out if his wife would train me for the contest. He assured me that she would be happy to help me and, indeed, she was most gracious in coaching me. Campus gossip had it that I could not hope to win because of my Southern drawl. This was news to me, since I had always assumed that the Southern drawl was uniquely the possession of Southern whites. However, the rumor intensified my determination to win, and I did, by the unanimous decision of the three judges. This victory gave me campus recognition by both faculty and students. After only eight weeks at Bates, I had won first prize in the sophomore declamation contest, and I was elated to have won over my eight white competitors. This early success of mine was not forgotten at the College; it was even mentioned in the commentary on me in my senior yearbook:

> Do you hear that rich mellow tone, that southern dialect? Who can it be with that enchanting ring to his voice, that clear deliberate enunciation to his oratory. That's Bennie Mays, and say can't he speak! If you hear him once you will always remember him. Bennie came to us in the fall of '17 and immediately made his name by running away with the sophomore prize decs. Since then, he has been in many speaking contests and debates.[1]

That contest was won on the Pullman cars of the New York Central Railroad, and through the coaching of Mrs. Fred Pomeroy and "Professor Rob," as Grosvenor May Robinson, professor of Speech at Bates, was affectionately called. Professor Robinson loved his work at Bates and loved the students. When he retired, he took bus rides and traveled long distances to visit his students.

I have always been deeply appreciative when people did things for me that they were in no way obligated to do. I shall never forget Mrs. Pomeroy, and as long as she was alive, I went to see her whenever I was in Lewiston. In the same way, I shall never forget Professor Levister at South Carolina State, who lent me seventeen dollars to buy a cap and uniform for my first job; Professor Nix, who made it possible for me to be graduated from high school in three years; Professors Wingfield and Hadley of Virginia Union, who interceded for me at Bates; the student who befriended me on the train while I was en route to Bates; and Julian Coleman, who extended himself to help me adjust at Bates, and who was as ecstatic as a child with a new toy when I won the declamation contest.

[1] Bates College, *The Mirror* (Class of 1920), page 48.

Let me list some others: there was my mathematics teacher, Professor Ramsey, who guided me through analytic geometry, calculus, and differential equations. He was competent in math, and he was kind. He was willing to vouch for me to do graduate work in mathematics at the University of Chicago, if I wanted him to. Though I took no course in geology and astronomy, Professor Tubb was able in these disciplines, and I sat in on his lectures. He was a man of conviction. He opposed our entering the First World War, inviting some alienation among his colleagues. Professor J. Murray Carroll was outstanding in his courses in sociology and economics. Carroll came by to see me at Morehouse en route from Florida to Maine, shortly after I became president of Morehouse.

My victory in the declamation contest also attracted the attention of A. Craig Baird, professor of English and debating coach. The same afternoon that I won first prize in the contest, Professor Baird visited my room to urge me to try out for the debating team. At first, I refused on the grounds that I needed all of my time for study, particularly since I had to do other work in order to meet expenses. But Baird did not accept "no" so easily. He went away, but in a day or two he was back. On the third time around, he convinced me that I should try to make the varsity debating team. He told me of the fine record Bates had made, the finest in the nation, having won fifty-four decisions out of sixty-four debates in recent years. Accordingly, I went out for the tryouts and made the team, although I did not participate in intercollegiate debate during my sophomore year. Professor Baird included one of my speeches in *Representative American Speeches*. Bates enabled me to know I could match my brain with the New England whites who came from all over New England and beyond. At Bates, two more teachers impressed me positively: Arthur Frederick Hertell, professor of French, nicknamed "Frenchie" by his students.

25

Though not the best student in French, I enjoyed the beauty of his perfect enunciation and pronunciation of the French language more than the French I learned. Professor William Henry Hartshorne, called "Moonie" by the students, held us spellbound as he read Shakespeare and explained its meaning to us. This experience made me love Shakespeare the way Miss Kanty made me love Paul Laurence Dunbar.

Chapter Four

Until I entered Bates, I had always been a "straight A" student. During my first semester at Bates, I made only one "A," and was embarrassed and chagrined to receive the first and only "D" in my whole academic career. This demeaning grade was incurred in European History, and I always felt that I did not deserve it and that the teacher was prejudiced. This I cannot prove, but I felt that way. When I went back to Bates, subsequently, no one could have been more gracious and kind to me than this professor. In the second semester, I made three B's and three A's. In my junior year, my record was ten A's, five B's, and three C's. In my senior year, I received eight A's, two B's, and one C. I was one of the fifteen to be graduated with honors. The teachers at Bates are definitely among those who have driven me on.

Amusingly enough, that solitary "A" that graced my first semester record was made in Greek, the subject that was most difficult for me and troubled me most. Paul Tilden, who was a student in that class, made me the object of his wrath and unkind amusement. I had particular difficulty with pronunciation, and whenever I recited, Paul Tilden had a good chuckle or laugh at my expense, so much so that Professor George Millet Chase rebuked him. His obvious contempt for my efforts was painfully embarrassing to me, but perhaps I should be grateful to him for intensifying my determination to master Greek. I can recall that

27

once, after his amusement had been especially exasperating, I studied Greek until midnight and got up at three o'clock in the morning to study more. I asked Professor Chase for a conference to discuss the difficulty I was having. He invited me to his home, analyzed the problem, made some suggestions, and assured me that I had the ability to do the job. Immediately I began to improve, and by the end of the semester, I had made an "A" in Greek. I was very curious to find out what my fun-making friend had made, and I was mean enough to gloat because he had made a "B". I must admit that his "B" never did become a source of sorrow for me! Later, my heckler became much more friendly and wanted us to study Greek together. It was a subject that was never easy for me, but by consistent diligent work, I was able to make one "B" and five "A's" in the six semesters in which I studied Greek at Bates. These good grades, however, did not endear the subject to me—they had been too hard-won—and I refused to teach Greek at Morehouse when I went there in 1921.

Surely, George M. Chase was one of those persons who said to me, "You have the brain and the ability to conquer stiff subjects." He felt it was prejudice that kept me from being elected to Phi Beta Kappa at graduation. It was he who presented me when I was inducted into the Bates chapter in 1935, the first Negro to be elected to Phi Beta Kappa at Bates. Though I do not wear the key often, every time I look at my Phi Beta Kappa key, I remember Professor Chase.

I confess that I was disappointed when I was not elected to Phi Beta Kappa at graduation; that honor came fifteen years later. It did not lessen my disappointment when several students and three professors expressed surprise that I was not among those elected. Two professors predicted that I would make Phi Beta Kappa in the future; another said that I would do quite as well in life as any of my Phi Beta Kappa classmates, or better. Their predictions were cold comfort at the time.

At first, I was inclined to blame racial prejudice for my failure, but I could not really justify that position. Five of my six semesters at Bates might well have been considered outstanding, but not the first one. I was objective enough to admit that although the problems of adjusting to a new physical, social, and emotional environment might well explain those low grades, this explanation could not erase or change them. Moreover, things had gone too well for me at Bates for me to make excuses by ascribing prejudice and discrimination to the Phi Beta Kappa committee. In order to be accurate on this point, I have reviewed the official transcript of my Bates record. In summary, as indicated on page 27, I made twenty-two A's, thirteen B's, six Cs, and one D. Though possibly these grades represent an A-minus average, I am sure that the six C's and the one "D" spoke loudly in that Phi Beta Kappa committee meeting. Then, too, I had spent only three years at Bates, and my "straight A" record at Virginia Union was not taken into account. It may appear that I have attached undue importance to my grades, but they were tremendously important to me, not just for themselves, but for the evidence I had promised myself to produce: that superiority and inferiority in academic achievement had nothing to do with color of skin. Only in New England, I had felt, could I get the evidence, and in New England, I had produced the proof.

As indicated previously, I made the debating team my first at Bates (sophomore year), but because there were already enough experienced debaters I was not called upon to participate at the outset. That was just as well, since it enabled me to strike my academic stride during the second semester. The junior year, however, was a great disappointment to me, for not once in that year did I get the chance to debate. It was customary at Bates for a varsity debater to try out each fall in order to make the team, but this was not an ordinary fall. Bates was eager to debate larger and more prestigious colleges, and the chance came in the fall of 1918, when Cornell agreed to debate a subject of their own choosing. Since they gave us only three weeks, there was no time for tryouts, but there were four debaters carried over from the year before. The rules were waived and three of the four students were chosen to debate Cornell. I was not one of the three. Immediately after the Cornell debate, which Bates won, the opportunity came for Bates to debate Harvard College, again on short notice. The debating committee chose the same three men who had defeated Cornell. This apparently deliberate exclusion of me from both debates made me furious. I believed then, and I believe now, that if all four debaters had been white, all four would have been used in the two debates. It may be that race had nothing to do with the selections, and it is difficult to prove that it did. It is even more difficult to believe that it did not.

Since my three debating colleagues had not been required to participate in the tryouts that fall, I stubbornly refused to participate in them, on the ground that my status was identical to that of my associates who had debated Cornell and Harvard. I won the battle and was continued on the squad without having to try out. However, the college against which I was scheduled to participate in debating that year withdrew from the contest; thus my junior year passed without my participation in intercollegiate debate. In my senior year, at last, I was the final speaker and captain of the Bates debating team, when it defeated Tufts College in the spring of 1920!

Besides being a varsity debater and winner of the sophomore declamation contest, I was among the finalists in both the junior and senior oratorical contests. My classmates elected me to be the class-day orator. I was a member of the YMCA cabinet and represented Bates at the Northfield YMCA Conference in 1919. The members of the Bates Forum and the Philhellenic Club elected me their president.

The social life at Bates was no particular concern of mine. I had gone there primarily for academic reasons. Then, too, when I entered Bates, I was engaged to be married and was corresponding almost daily with Ellen Harvin, who had become my fiancée before I was graduated from high school and whom I married two months after my college graduation, August, 1920, in Newport News, Virginia. Ellen was in summer school at Hampton, Virginia. She died two years after our marriage. There were fewer than fifty Negroes in Lewiston and only one Negro girl, whom the Negro men at Bates seemed to like very much. Unfortunately, she was the girl friend of a jealous Portuguese, and we, therefore, kept our distance. Nevertheless, I became friends with many of my female and male classmates and have kept in touch with some of them through the years.

There was only one time during my three years at Bates that I experienced physical fear. Thomas Dixon's novel, *The Klansman*, had been made into a motion picture and released under the title *Birth of a Nation*. Along with other Negro students at Bates, I went to see it. It was a vicious, cynical, and completely perverted characterization of Negroes. Even in Maine, the picture aroused violent emotions and stirred up racial prejudice. Certain parts of it evoked violent words and threats from the audience. My fellow Negro students and I were not sure that we would be able to get back to the campus unmolested, but we did. This was my only experience with a prejudiced and hostile audience during my years in Lewiston. As those of us who are older may recall, this vile picture, despite protests by Negroes, was shown throughout the United States. The author of the book, Thomas Dixon, was a minister in North Carolina on Sundays; at other times, he devoted his mediocre talents to writing books designed to inflame prejudice between Negroes and whites, as well as between whites and Asians.

I spent three wonderful years at Bates. I have related some of my disappointments, but they were nothing compared to the rich harvest I gleaned from my association with the Bates faculty and students. I still knew no white Southerners whom I considered my friends, but I had made many Northern friends at Bates, and my attitude toward race was undergoing a tremendous change. Most of my professors are dead, but as long as they were alive, I was delighted in calling on them whenever I returned to Lewiston.

Many of my dreams came true at Bates, but foremost, through competitive experience, I had finally dismissed from my mind, for all time, the myth of the inherent inferiority of all Negroes and the inherent superiority of all whites—articles of faith to so many in my previous environment. I had done better in academic performance, in public speaking, and in argument and debate than the vast majority of my classmates. I concede academic superiority to not more than four in my class. I had displayed more initiative as a student leader than the majority of my classmates. Bates College made these experiences possible. Bates College did not "emancipate" me; it did far greater service of making it possible for me to emancipate myself and to accept with dignity my own worth as a free man. Small wonder that I love Bates College! It was a moving and wonderful experience to return there in 1970, for my fiftieth class reunion.[1]

I learned, after going to Bates, the folly of making

[1] On June 6–8, 1980, I attended the sixtieth reunion of my college class (1920) at Bates. There were thirteen of us present.

final judgments without thorough investigation, solely on the basis of reading catalogs—catalogs of Brown and Dartmouth. I finished Bates four years after high-school graduation. At the time I left State in Orangeburg, however, having been frightened away from trying to enter Brown or Dartmouth, I decided that I would spend a year in a Northern prep school and then seek admission to some New England college. I wrote to several such schools, but I received little or no encouragement from any one of them. The one reply that I received had the virtue of honesty but, nonetheless, was disappointing and dispiriting. The Reverend Lorin Webster, L.H.D., rector of Holderness School in New Hampshire, stated clearly that he could not take me because of my race. Quite often, Northern schools "put it on the South" when they refused to accept Negro students, but the rector of Holderness School "told it like it was." I have kept Mr. Webster's letter:

> Camp Wachusett
> Holderness School
> Portsmouth, New Hampshire
> The Reverend Lorin Webster, L.H.D.
> Rector

Mr. B. E. Mays
107 West 132 Street
New York City

> July 31, 1916

My dear Sir:
    I wish I could help you in your laudable desire to get an education, but if I should admit a boy of your race to Holderness School I should lose several students. So I am obliged to decline to receive you.[2]

> Very truly yours,
> L. Webster

[2]Holderness School has long since abandoned the policy of racial exclusiveness.

I had already met Northern prejudice in a small way in New York in 1915, and also in Detroit. Now I had met it in the Holderness School in New Hampshire, in a letter that banished all hope that I might be able to enter a Northern college in September of 1916.

While I had been licensed for the ministry in 1919 (I was ordained two years later, in 1921), I came to my senior year in college still undecided about my future plans. I was not as sure as I had been in my earlier years when the pastor and church people at Mount Zion had predicted that I would preach.

Professor Halbert Haine Britan told me that he could get me a fellowship to study at the University of Chicago in the Department of Philosophy. I had done well in mathematics and had given some thought to doing graduate work in that field, but knowing my interest in religion, Professor Herbert Howell Purinton, my teacher in religion, was ready to speak for me at Newton Theological Seminary and recommend me to Dean Shailer Mathews, dean of the Divinity School at the University of Chicago. Religion finally won out over both philosophy and mathematics.

Although I had set my sight on the University of Chicago during my high-school days, I was interested in hearing about Newton Theological Seminary. In the spring of 1920, when the Newton "scout" came to Bates recruiting students, he made it quite plain that Newton was not interested in Negro students and advised me to go for my theological training to Virginia Union University, where I had spent my freshman college year. I came to realize that it was not only Holderness School that didn't want Negroes; the famous Newton Theological Seminary was similarly prejudiced. Professor Purinton assured me that I need feel no concern over Newton's closed doors, since the University of Chicago was superior to Newton.

Bates meant much to me, but I was not satisfied. I wanted to go to the University of Chicago to compete with white men from across the United States, from all races, all classes, and all national backgrounds. Having done so, I found more people who drove me on. My major professor was Edwin E. Aubrey, professor of Christian Theology and Ethics. My courses in that department were just about equally divided between Aubrey and Henry Nelson Wieman. My philosophy courses and philosophy of religion courses were taken with Wieman. Aubrey was hard, and his former students advised me to avoid him. Shailer Mathews advised me to take Aubrey's courses, and I took them. When I got an "A" in Aubrey's first course, I was delighted, and I continued to make A's in other courses.

Chapter Five

As indicated on pages 10 and 12, my choice of the University of Chicago for graduate work was largely determined by the influence of N. C. Nix, one of my high-school teachers at State College. He influenced me more than any other teacher at State College. It was he who made me vow that some day I would be a student at the University of Chicago, though he attended only summer school at the university. The following developments occurred soon after my graduation from Bates: I married Ellen Harvin in Newport News, Virginia, in August of 1920, and my bride returned to South Carolina to teach. Ellen died two years later. I went North to work as a Pullman porter that fall, hoping to earn enough to pay a few debts, and to save enough to enter the Divinity School of the University of Chicago in January 1921. When January came, however, I was no more financially able to matriculate in the University of Chicago than I had been to enter Bates in the fall of 1917. I had arrived at Bates with ninety dollars in my pocket; I landed in Chicago with forty-five dollars.

Although I had worked in the Pullman service for several summers and had a good record, I was fired in Boston in December 1920. I had hoped to work my way to Chicago as a Pullman porter, so that I would have at least forty or fifty dollars on arrival. Two things were responsible for my being fired. Boston was my headquarters and the district out of which I worked. It was customary not to pay a porter when he was being held for service in his home district. If things were slack and a porter couldn't get an assignment, he received no pay, even if ten or more days passed before any work developed. On the other hand, a New York porter in Boston, for example, would be paid. Porters who were not regularly in the employ of the Pullman Company resented this partiality. Some local officials tried to save the Pullman Company money by detaining their own men for special service, while giving assignments to porters from other districts.

Either in October or November, Harvard played football against Yale in New Haven. The Boston porters who came into Boston any day of that week, Monday through Friday, were held there to guarantee that there would be enough porters to service the parlor cars that would be needed for fans going to the Harvard-Yale football game. Several Boston porters came in on Monday, and instead of being sent out again, they were told to report on Saturday to go to New Haven. Porters from other districts who came into Boston that week were assigned out. The Boston porters protested, to no avail, and a group of us decided to make out our own time slips, sending a letter to the Pullman superintendent in Chicago, explaining the situation and requesting pay for the week. Chicago authorized Boston to pay us. Our signatures had appeared only on the time slips; however, since I was the only college man in the group, the Pullman officials in Boston immediately suspected me of initiating the appeal to Chicago. The porters had previously agreed that the group was responsible, rather than any one person, but although no one was fired for this incident, my name had become suspect.

Later, I had an altercation with a Pullman conductor. Early one morning, around six o'clock, I was to discharge a passenger at Syracuse. While he dressed, I put his bed away so that he would have a place to sit until his arrival in Syracuse. Just as my passenger got off, a gentleman came up and asked me whether I had a seat to Buffalo. I said "yes." When I told the conductor, he replied that I had no space. I explained, telling him that the diagram would show that I had put one passenger off at Syracuse. The conductor kept insisting that I had no space; and even if I had discharged a passenger, the berth had not been put away. I was equally insistent because it was I who had put the berth away. The conductor and I exchanged "hot" words. He said that he was going to report me. Since the conductor was the porter's superior officer, a black mark from him could spell disaster, and it did. The conductor carried out his threat; he reported me to the Boston superintendent and my firing was imminent.

Christmas was close at hand, and I had to make the trip to South Carolina to see Ellen, my wife, whom I had not seen since our marriage in August. I did see her in Columbia, South Carolina, but my plans to go to Chicago from Columbia fell apart. I had had it all planned. I had expected to work as a Pullman porter from Columbia, hoping to pick up a little money in tips en route to Chicago. I was unable to get any work out of Columbia. Instead, I was given an assignment on a "deadhead" car that was connected to a slow-moving freight train. When a Pullman car was not in service, a porter was sent along to protect it, and this was called a "deadhead" car.

In Richmond, I learned that my deadhead car had been assigned to Pittsburgh rather than to Washington. I tried to get an assignment to Chicago out of Richmond, but with no success. I decided to beg the train conductor to let me go from Richmond to Washington on my Pullman keys. Kindly conductors occasionally permitted this, and luckily this conductor consented. Cheered by his consideration, I had hopes that Washington would assign me to a car bound for Chicago. I almost made it! The slip assigning me to Chicago had been put into my hand, and then I was told, "Wait a minute!" The assignment clerk went through some letters and told me that since I was wanted in Boston, he would have to send me there. As soon as I got to Boston, the man in the yard office told me that the superintendent wanted to see me. I knew what was coming. It took few words for the superintendent to tell me that I was fired, and he demanded the immediate return of my keys.

This was on Friday, December 31, 1920. I had forty-seven dollars in my pocket, and a thousand miles separated me from the University of Chicago. I told Bryant, a porter who was my friend, about my plight. I explained how much I wanted to enroll in the University of Chicago on Monday, January 3, 1921. I was talking to the right man, for he wanted to help me. Bryant and I had worked on adjacent cars going to Buffalo one summer day. He became sick and found himself unable to serve his passengers; so I had taken care of his car as well as my own. In Buffalo, Bryant had to be taken to a hospital. After putting away his car and mine, I went to the hospital to see my friend and took him the $13.60 his passengers had given me in tips. When I explained my predicament to Bryant, he was eager to help me, again expressing his appreciation for my earlier kindness to him. Bryant had an assignment out of Springfield, Massachusetts, for Cleveland, on New Year's night. First he offered to give me his assignment to Cleveland, but we both realized that he would lose his job if he did so. Next he offered to take a chance and let me deadhead with him to Springfield, Massachusetts, and from Springfield to help me hide from the conductor, until we got to Cleveland.

I was to join Bryant on his deadhead car at Back Bay Station, but Bryant's deadhead car was hitched to a fast train that did not stop at Back Bay. When the train came whizzing through Back Bay, it was literally flying. Bryant was on the platform of his car waving frantically, and I was left standing on the platform of the station, holding my bags. This was on Saturday night, January 1, 1921. I was due to register at the University of Chicago on Monday morning, January 3.

I decided to pay my way on the next train from Back Bay to Springfield and to look for my friend, who was not to leave Springfield for Cleveland until late that New Year's night. My ticket cost me $3.17. When I found Bryant in Springfield, making down his beds, I put on a white coat to help him finish the job and receive his passengers. This was all very well, but how was I to get to Cleveland without the conductor's discovering me and pulling me off that train? Bryant and I agreed that I would evade the conductor by getting behind him, as he went through the train checking his passengers and collecting tickets. When a conductor checked his passengers, he usually took a seat somewhere and made up his record. While the conductor was preparing his records, Bryant hid me in a vacant upper berth, and there I slept until late the next morning. Somewhere between Rochester and Buffalo, when Bryant was sure the conductor was not around, he awakened me.

I dressed and Bryant stowed me away in the linen closet. To keep me from suffocating, he put a cord on the door so that it wouldn't slam and lock. To protect me further, he placed the soiled linen bag in front of me. Twice the conductor came to that closet for something, but I was securely hidden. Thus concealed and barricaded, I rode into Cleveland, where Bryant's car terminated. This was Sunday night, January 2. Registration at the University of Chicago was less than twelve hours away, and I was still three hundred miles from Chicago.

Luck was still with me! When I got to Cleveland, the man in charge of the Pullman service was short of porters. He needed someone to man a car to Toledo. I explained that I had to register the next morning at the University of Chicago and pleaded with him to send me to Chicago. I had been fired and was no longer in the employ of the Pullman Company but, fortunately, another set of keys was in my pocket. How I got them, I do not now know. (My mother, perhaps, would have considered them an answer to her prayers!) The Cleveland man was sympathetic and told me that he had a porter coming in who was really too tired to go to Toledo. If I would make down the car and put the passengers to bed so that the tired porter, due thirty minutes before the Chicago train was scheduled to leave, could go to bed and get some rest, he would send me to Chicago as a swing man. A porter was called "a swing man" when he was sent along to help, but was not in charge of the car. I was only too happy to accept this offer. I arrived in Chicago at eight o'clock in the morning, on January 3.

Luck was still on my side. I had my forty-three dollars in my pocket. Thanks to Bryant, I had eaten each meal between Springfield and Cleveland. I registered on the day of my arrival in Chicago, found a place to live a few blocks from the university, and secured a job washing dishes in the Commons. There was virtually no tuition to be paid at the Divinity School. I got my meals in return for washing dishes, and, if I remember correctly, I got paid something besides.

Chapter Six

Finally, at long last, I was registered at the University of Chicago, about which N. C. Nix had bragged so much, and of which I had dreamed so often. I was now destined to come into contact with some of the world's greatest scholars. Despite my extremely conservative background and orthodox religious upbringing, the ultramodern views of the University of Chicago scholars did not upset my faith. What they taught made sense to me. The professors in the Divinity School believed that in order to understand the chapters in the Old and New Testaments, one would need to know the social, economic, political, and religious background out of which the Bible was written. Thus, the men were inspired, but they were not infallible. For example, illustrations and parables were used to show that the Bible did not have to be taken literally in order for it to be true.

I found more prejudice at the University of Chicago and in the city of Chicago than I had found at Bates and in the city of Lewiston, Maine. There was much less prejudice, bias, and discrimination, of course, than I had found in Greenwood County, South Carolina. At the University, Negro men could live in Goodspeed Hall, but only because Goodspeed was the dormitory reserved for graduate students in the Divinity School. Most southern students, and some northern students, would not eat at the same table with Negroes. Negro students, therefore, took great delight in increasing the physical acitivity of the prejudiced, by causing them to change tables quite frequently! In the University Commons, where the majority of the students ate, the service was cafeteria-style, so that persons went through the line, selected food, and sat wherever they chose or where there was space. Those persons who would not eat at a table with Negroes were soon spotted. Many times, I saw white men and women, halfway through their meals, take up plates, silver, and glassware and move to a table where there were no Negroes. Some of us took pleasure in plaguing these people by deliberately seating ourselves at a table where some white person had fled to escape eating with Negroes. I recall one man who moved three times to avoid the Negro students that followed him from table to table. Finally, with ill-concealed disgust, he left without finishing his meal.

At Bates, teachers spoke to Negro students on campus and downtown, especially if the Negro student was in the professor's class. Lewiston restaurants were open to Negro students without discrimination. Not so in Chicago in 1921! Most of the restaurants, perhaps, all, in the vicinity of the University of Chicago denied service to Negroes. Interesting and stimulating though the University of Chicago was, it was not quite the "heaven" Professor Nix's fond recollection had painted, at least not with regard to racial equality.

Aubrey suggested that I do my thesis with him, although I had talked with Wieman about a subject for my thesis. I found myself in a dilemma, but Wieman made it easy for me. He stated that he thought my thesis should be with Aubrey. I was delighted to hear Aubrey say publicly, in a meeting that we were attending, that he sponsored me, voted for me to receive the Ph.D. and that he would do it again, if he had the chance. Aubrey was an able teacher, and I wished that someday I could lecture with the clarity of Doctor Aubrey. We remained friends until Dr. Aubrey's death. Every Christmas, Mrs. Aubrey and I exchange greetings.

Henry Nelson Wieman whetted my appetite further for exploration into philosophy. He led the class through the works of Alfred North Whitehead, an eminent Harvard philosopher. It was sad to have Wieman tell me on one of my visits to see him that he felt that his life had been a failure. He felt that he had left nothing for posterity. I pointed out that as a student of his, I knew that he would live on with me and his other students. His books and articles would be read by generations to come; researchers would be studying his theology and philosophy. Today, even if Wieman's image has faded, it will come up again. I can understand Wieman's position. For a while, he was perhaps the most talked-about theologian-philosopher in the country. *The Christian Century* did much to make him known to the people of this country. The feeling of defeat that he expressed to me may be common to all of us. I have come to the conclusion that one should do his best and leave his image to God and the people.

There was Doctor Soares who was a popular preacher, especially among the women's colleges of the East. Black students thought that Professor Soares was arrogant and biased where blacks were involved. He wore a preacher's long coat and a derby hat. Soares did not speak to his students when he met them on the campus. However, when Professor Soares was with his wife, and met us on the street, we called him by name and tipped our hats. Of course, he had to respond with a greeting of some kind.

Doctor J.M.P. Smith, chairman of the Department of Old Testament, was an able scholar. He was a powerful lecturer, as clear as crystal. I thought he was prejudiced against Negroes, but I had no proof of this. I was able to get only a "B," never an "A" from Smith. If one did the reading required and digested the many books asigned in the course, he did well. In addition, there was no reason for him or her not to do well, if he did the research paper that was required in every course in the Divinity School.

Professor Willett was another excellent lecturer on the Old Testament, and my record was excellent in his course. Shailer Mathews, dean of the Divinity School, was not as easily understood in his lectures as others, but he made up for this by allowing more questions and discussions. Dean Shirley Jackson Case was a man who walked straight, stood erect, and kept a stern face. There was little discussion in his class, but I made A's in his courses. His concentration was in Early Christianity. My master's thesis was written in his department, and he was my adviser. My thesis was entitled "The Survival of Pagan Religion in Early Christianity." It was in connection with my thesis that I learned that Dean Case was kind. After completing writing my master's thesis, I left the manuscript with Dr. Case to read. When he had finished the reading, he sent for me. He made a few minor suggestions, but I was afraid that he was not going to accept it as final. Observing my fear and nervousness, he said: "Mr. Mays, don't be upset, I am going to approve the thesis. You have done a good job." When I defended my thesis for the Ph.D. degree, I was sitting among six professors in the Divinity School, and Dean Case was one of them. I defended the thesis with no difficulty. While the committee was discussing my defense, Dean Case asked Aubrey if I were coming back to get my Ph.D. degree. This peeved Aubrey and he snapped at the dean, saying, "Knowing Mays, as I do, he would not make that decision until I told him he had passed the examination."

There were three other interesting comments on my Ph.D. thesis examination that struck me as significant. Professor Kinchloe, who had told me that I could never get a thesis out of the subject I had chosen, retracted his statement and congratulated me when he heard the defense. Doctor Donald Riddle of the New Testament Department told Aubrey that he would have been proud if I had written that thesis in his department. When I returned to the university in 1932, I had written my first book, *The Negro's Church*. I was told by a third friend, Dick Edwards, that I had better try to get my doctor's thesis out of that book. He suggested that if I did not get my thesis out of that study, I would not complete the doctorate. Of course, no university would accept a thesis that that school did not supervise. I did not use that book as a thesis, and I did get the doctorate. While I was in the Divinity School, 40 percent of the doctoral candidates failed their final written examinations, and never got their theses accepted.

Another fine man taught me during a summer quarter in a course on "The Authority and Prestige of the Catholic Church." As I recall, his name was Sullivan. That course awakened in me an appreciation for the Catholic Church, which was helpful to me when I was appointed by President John Kennedy as one of four Americans to attend the state funeral of Pope John XXIII. All the students in the course on Catholicism were required to write a final paper on the same subject. When Professor Sullivan returned the papers, he told the class that the best one, from a class of approximately twenty students, was turned in by Benjamin Mays. That evening, I had a visitor. He wasn't hesitant at all in displaying his prejudice against blacks. He said that he wanted to see a paper written by a Negro that Professor Sullivan said was "the best." I handed him the paper and, after reading it, he said to me, "It's a pretty good paper." I replied that Professor Sullivan thought it was excellent. I asked him what he had made.

He replied, "I got a 'B'." I replied, "Good." He said he had never known an intelligent Negro before.

"There were a few in my town, but I never knew them." This incident is one of my personal experiences that can document how divisive and cruel segregation was at the time.

One of the most fascinating courses I ever took at the University of Chicago was with a man whose theology I rejected. The man was A. E. Hayden, a humanist. He would sweep away all angels, Jesus Christ, God, heaven, and hell. As I recall it now, Doctor Hayden believed that man could build a world of peace, goodwill, and justice without relying on the traditional Christian theology. I was attracted to him because of his firm belief in humankind and the fervor with which he defended his position. He did it with the zeal of the old-time Baptist preacher, of the kind that I had heard in my Baptist community in South Carolina. I heard him say in Rockefeller Chapel that "The life of one child is more important than all of the buildings put up on the can·pus of the university." I said that if this man thought like that, I would take as many courses as I could with him, without neglecting the courses required in my major. Hayden was a handsome, scholarly, and kind man. I liked him and he liked me, and he seemed to enjoy my questions, attacking his position. He became a part of my life—a beautiful man, indeed. He has driven me on.

How could I forget J. Edgar Goodspeed and J. DeWitt Burton, both professors in the New Testament Department. Goodspeed was scholarly, gentle, and kind. He was noted for his translation of the New Testament into Modern English, but no man was more impressive than Burton. Each person in the class was assigned sections in the New Testament and was required to report to the whole class from time to time. Burton was one of my ablest teachers throughout my whole academic career. Every time he called upon me to recite, I was "scared." When he got through expanding on what I had done, I feared that I had flunked the course. In the final examination, he framed questions to cover the entire course. I was naturally surprised and happy when I received an "A" from Dr. Burton.

I liked Burton, because he always spoke to me and called me by name. He had lifted the ban of restriction that kept Negro students from using the recreational facilities in Reynolds Hall, when he was acting president of the university, after the death of the current president. During that time, I am told that he mapped out the expansion for the university that served as a guide for years to come. It is reported that when Burton, at a board meeting, revealed his plans for the university, his work had been so thorough and his plan so comprehensive that the trustee board made him president of the university. I received my M.A. degree during Burton's presidency. Unfortunately, he died before all his plans for the university were realized.

The next president, Robert Maynard Hutchins, was a lawyer. He came to the university at the age of thirty-one, perhaps the youngest president in the history of great universities. He was deemed a radical in the field of higher education, and was thought by many to be a genius. It is alleged that he was loved by many of the faculty members and strongly disliked by others. He instituted bold experiments; for example, if a student from high school could pass the entrance examination, he was admitted to the Ph.D. program. Hutchins abolished football and made other striking changes that affected the direction of the university for many years. I received my Ph.D. under Hutchins. I love the Hutchins family, whom I considered to be my friends. Doctor William J. Hutchins came from a professorship at Oberlin to Berea as president. His son, Francis, succeeded his father, Robert Maynard, as president. I remember visiting Berea college in the early sixties, when William J. Hutchins was ill. From that illness, he never recovered.

Chapter Seven

The further I moved up the academic ladder, the more I felt obligated to all the people who had touched my life and had driven me on. As I look back, I am more and more convinced that no man is self-made. Yes, one is due credit for his ability to "fight it out," despite crippling circumstances, and for using his mind, but God and his parents gave him his mind. Any man who says he is self-made tells an untruth. In addition to God and parents, one is indebted to all of those people who gave him a helping hand and an encouraging word. "No man is an island entire of himself." No man, however high he may ascend, has the right to look down with condescension upon another person. He, too, might have been poor and illiterate. He, too, might have suffered the same fate—but for the grace of God!

Even those people who have made a negative impact on my life have been a part of the forces that have driven me on. They showed me what I must *not* become. I was determined that I would not let the lynching mob and the brutal treatment I received at the hands of white people beat me down. I would not let a drunkard, a dope addict, or a thief make me follow in his footsteps. If I did, he would determine the destiny of my life. Even these unfortunate ones are a part of that group that has driven me on, showing me what I must *not* become.

It should be interesting to the reader to follow me in my early travels abroad, for the people I met there are among those who have improved my life and also have driven me on. My first trip abroad came in 1937, when I was one of thirteen Americans to be chosen by the National Council of the Y.M.C.A. to attend its world convention in Mysore, India. I had never been outside the United States, and the National Council had given me, and the other twelve in the group, time to spend eight or ten days visiting London and Paris, Palestine and Egypt, and Bombay, before the conference started in Mysore, where the all-India Congress was in session. There I met three very important people: Nehru; Mrs. Pandit, Nehru's sister; and Mahatma Gandhi. I hired an interpreter who spoke English to tell me what was being said in the Hindi language. After hearing what the speakers were saying, I concluded that the days of the British in India were numbered. I did not see Gandhi at the Congress because he went to his tent to engage in his evening prayers. His secretary explained that he could not see me then, but if I could come to Warda, not far from Bombay, he would arrange for me to have an extended conference with the Mahatma. This was good advice. When I went to Warda, I had an opportunity to talk with him for ninety minutes—one of the truly great experiences in my life. Physically, Gandhi was not impressive; he weighed only ninety pounds. But mentally, spiritually, and morally, he was a giant of a man. I told him that I had elected to visit him instead of taking a trip to see the Taj Mahal. He replied that I had chosen wisely, because if I came to India again, he would probably be dead. He was right. When my wife Sadie and I visited India in 1952, to attend the meeting of the Central Committee of the World Council of Churches in Lucknow, Gandhi had been assassinated.

Gandhi, a low-caste man, a graduate from the University of London, never tried to identify himself with the English. After a sojourn in South Africa, he returned to India to lead the battle for India's independence and succeeded. He and Nehru lifted the British Empire off its hinges.

Gandhi made a great impression on Martin Luther King, Jr. When a student at Morehouse, Martin heard Mordecai Johnson tell about Gandhi's work. And after that, he became an avid reader of Gandhi's work. Martin brought the Gandhian philosophy to the United States and made it applicable in his own activities, as he waged his campaign against racism in our country.

There is no way I could have been given the opportunities to attend these conferences without the support of people who saw in me those qualities that would enable me to make a contribution to the cause of justice and equality. There was Channing Tobias, whom I knew when I was a high school student at the State College in Orangeburg, South Carolina. I am indebted to him for several things. It was Tobias who recommended that I become the National YMCA secretary, with the responsibility for visiting colleges and YMCAs in South Carolina, Georgia, Florida, Alabama, and Tennessee. It was Tobias who was responsible for my visit to India as one of thirteen Americans to participate in the World YMCA Conference in Mysore, India, in 1937. This led to other international travel, as a delegate to conferences in Sweden and Switzerland. It was Tobias who recommended me to Mordecai Johnson as one worthy to be the first Negro dean of the School of Religion at Howard University. Tobias was an able man, eloquent in speech and adamant in doing everything that he could do to make the letter "C" (Christian) functional in the YMCA. I believe that if he had been white, he would have been the head man in the YMCA in this country (at that time). Tobias opened the way for me, and he, along with many friends in the YMCA across the world, is among the host of people who have inspired me and "driven me on." They are a part of my life and have helped to make me what I am today. My speaking and preaching in churches, colleges, and universities were partly responsible for my being elected vice-president of the Federal Council of Churches of Christ in 1946, under Bishop Oxnam. He was elected president of the Federal Council of Churches at the same time that I was elected in Pittsburgh, Pennsylvania. This position brought invitations to me from city councils of churches, councils in the Midwest, New York, Pennsylvania, Maryland, North Carolina, Virginia, and many other places. When the Federal Council merged with other denominations into the National Council of Churches of Christ, the stage was set for my being a part of the World Council of Churches, which was organized in Amsterdam, Holland, in 1948. Frankly, I was not aware that I was becoming the most widely known black churchman in the United States. I did not seek this position; it was thrust upon me.

At Amsterdam, as a delegate from the National Baptist Convention, I never dreamed that I would be elected one of the ninety persons who were to form the Central Committee, one that carried on the work of the World Council between world assemblies. The truth of the matter is, I tried my best, when nominated, not to serve. The names of the ninety members were printed and posted twenty-four hours before the vote. When Reverend Aubrey, head of the Baptist organization in England and chairman of the committee to select the ninety members, came to me for a recommendation from the National Baptist Convention, I insisted that a pastor in the National Baptist Convention should be the man. When he asked me whom I would recommend, I suggested Doctor J. H. Jackson of the Olivet Baptist Church in Chicago. When he came back to me, he said that the committee had nominated me for membership on the Central Committee.

I began then to take my role more seriously, not just as a member, a body filling space, but as one who had to make an impact in conferences where world problems and issues were discussed. I had spoken in plenary sessions, making changes as well as additions in sessions on race and economic justice. I engaged in these discussions because I thought that a world assembly should speak prophetically to the world. Even then, I said to my delegation that I should not be the person, but to no avail. I was unanimously elected along with the rest. Representatives from Communist Russia could not come to Amsterdam; therefore, places were reserved for them, and we operated with eighty members, minus the ten Russians.

Chapter Eight

I cannot neglect to make special mention of my three years as a teacher at Morehouse and my twenty-seven years as its president. The experiences of these thirty years have driven me on. Morehouse men, though few in number when compared to the vast numbers in big colleges, have done exceptionally well. If a college is to maintain a high level of academic excellence, it must have not only an able faculty and a good plant, but also a majority of able students. In the final analysis, a college or university must be judged by the achievements of its alumni. On this score, Morehouse College has a proud record.

Within recent years, a high percentage of the graduates of Morehouse have gone on to graduate and professional schools. In 1964, 52 percent of Morehouse graduates entered graduate and professional schools; in 1966, 51.5 percent. In 1967, the number went as high as 56 percent. In the six-year span between 1961 and 1967, Morehouse seniors were awarded eighty-nine fellowships and assistantships to graduate and professional schools. In 1967, Morehouse graduates were studying in forty-five of the best graduate and professional schools in the nation. It is also significant that, between 1945 and 1967, Morehouse stood second among Georgia institutions in the production of Woodrow Wilson fellows.

By 1967, 118 Morehouse graduates had earned

Ph.D. degrees. In 1967, one of every eighteen Negroes earning doctorates had received the A.B. or B.S. degree from Morehouse. This figure is marvelous on two counts: Not more than 4,000 men had been graduated from Morehouse. Moreover, Earl J. McGrath, in his book *The Predominantly Negro Colleges and Universities in Transition* (Columbia University, 1965), reports that there were 123 predominantly Negro colleges in this country. In addition, Negroes have been graduating from white colleges since the first Negro graduated from Bowdoin College in 1826. The one-to-eighteen ratio has hardly changed; since 1967, many more Morehouse graduates have earned doctorates. These degrees have been earned in the last thirty-seven years, for it was in 1932 that Samuel Milton Nabrit, Morehouse '25, became the first, when he received the Ph.D. from Brown University. Between 1932 and 1967, Morehouse had averaged three and one-half Ph.D.'s a year.

Morehouse men have received doctorates from forty-five different universities between 1932 and 1967. Such a record is hardly an accident. It is a tradition at Morehouse that an A.B. or B.S. is not a terminal degree; every outstanding student is encouraged to continue his studies. It should also be noted that many of the Morehouse men who have earned doctorates were early-admission students, who came to Morehouse as freshmen after completing the tenth or eleventh grades of high school. Morehouse started its early-admissions program before the Ford Foundation initiated a similar program. With Morehouse, it was a method of survival. World War II so diminished the Morehouse enrollment that the chairman of the Board suggested closing the college for the duration. Actually, nobody took the chairman seriously; but we did get busy recruiting bright young students who had not finished high school. Among those so recruited was Martin Luther King, Jr., Class of '48.

Morehouse stands among the first four Negro institutions in the production of graduates who go on to medical and dental training and careers. By 1967, more than three hundred Morehouse men had earned M.D.'s and D.D.S.'s, and forty of the three hundred achieved distinction as medical specialists—diplomates in medicine. A high percentage of all Negro physicians did their undergraduate work at Morehouse College. When the degrees in medicine and the Ph.D.'s are combined, it is apparent that one out of every nine Morehouse graduates had earned an academic or professional doctorate. There are several reasons that many Negro men have chosen medical careers: Medicine is a prestigious field. Income is good. For a long time, only a few professions were open to blacks—preaching, teaching, and medicine. As a physician or dentist, a Negro could be his own boss. Negroes looked up to their doctors; and even prejudiced whites had respect for Negro doctors.

For many years Morehouse men have been holding administrative and teaching positions in Negro and white colleges and universities. In 1967, Morehouse graduates were teachers and administrators in fifty-eight predominantly black institutions and twenty-two white institutions. Twenty-one institutions of higher learning have had or now have Morehouse men as their presidents; and these presidents have served these twenty-one institutions for a total of 309 years.

When Morehouse celebrated its one-hundredth anniversary in 1967, the college had assistant superintendents of public schools in San Diego, Detroit, and Gary, Indiana. Five of the seven principals of the predominantly Negro high schools in Atlanta were Morehouse men; and Morehouse men were and continue to be teaching in the public schools throughout the nation. In the field of music, too, Morehouse training has been outstanding. The best glee club in the nation is trained by Wendell P. Whalum, Sr. There were in 1979 forty Morehouse men in leadership positions in the Atlanta Public School system: namely, seven resource coordinators, ten assistant principals, sixteen principals, four directors, one area superintendent, one assistant superintendent, and one associate superintendent.

The early emphasis on religion and the later emphasis on the arts and sciences did not lessen Morehouse's interest in preparing men for the ministry. The Morehouse School of Religion is one of the six institutions that make up the Interdenominational Theological Center. Today, Morehouse graduates are pastors of Negro churches in twenty-one large cities. In addition to these pastorates, Morehouse men have achieved distinction in other fields of religion. Among these men are Howard Thurman, listed several years ago by *Life* magazine as one of the twelve great preachers in the United States, and who was Dean of the Chapel at Boston University for more than a decade; the Right Reverend Dillard H. Brown was Episcopal Bishop of Liberia; Dr. Thomas Kilgore was the first black minister to become president of the American Baptist Convention; George Kelsey, professor at Drew Theological Seminary, who influenced the immortal Martin Luther King, Jr., to enter the ministry and was both a great civil-rights leader and a compelling pulpiteer. Two Morehouse men, William Sterling Cary and Moses William Howard, Jr., have served as presidents of the National Council of Churches.

The first Negro daily newspaper in the nation, *The Atlanta Daily World*, was founded by a Morehouse man, W. A. Scott, Sr., and its present editor, C. A. Scott, is a Morehouse man. Lerone Bennett, senior editor of *Ebony*, is without a doubt one of the leading editorial writers in the nation, and a Morehouse man. *Life* magazine went out of business several years ago because it was in financial difficulty. They are back now as a monthly, and I believe they took a clue from the way *Ebony* magazine carries on its work. Bob Johnson, associate editor of *Jet* magazine, which is perhaps the most profitable magazine in any of the Johnson Publications, is a Morehouse man. Other Morehouse men who are authors of note are James Birnie, Benjamin Brawley, George Kelsey, Martin Luther King, Jr., Ira de A. Reid, Howard Thurman, B. R. Brazel, Frank Forbes, E. A. Jones, N. P. Tillman, Hugh Gloster, Charles Willie, Russell Adams, Billy Joe Evans, and Walter Massey.

Morehouse men are serving admirably in responsible positions in banking and insurance institutions across the country, and Morehouse graduates are creditably represented among the ever-increasing number of young blacks now employed and sought for employment by white financial institutions. Although it is not possible to determine at this writing all the places Morehouse men are in industry, it is known that they are serving well in many of the nation's giant firms: pilots with American Airlines and one with Southern, Eastern and Delta. Successful men of Morehouse have driven me on.

It took from 1952 to 1966 to persuade representatives of Phi Beta Kappa to visit Morehouse to determine whether we qualified for membership. In August 1967, the United Chapters of Phi Beta Kappa, meeting at Duke University, voted to admit Morehouse College to membership. Only seven other institutions in the nation were selected that year. Since we wanted the president of Phi Beta Kapa to install the chapter, we postponed the installation until January 6, 1968. Thus, Delta of Georgia was established at Morehouse, rewarding fourteen years of effort. The installation ceremonies were impressive. Phi Beta Kappa members from other chapters in Georgia, the presidents of the other five institutions in the Atlanta University Center, the trustees of Morehouse College, and some of the outstanding high-school students in the public schools of Atlanta were present.

On Friday, May 17, 1968, Delta of Georgia was proud to initiate into Phi Beta Kappa the first Morehouse students to qualify for membership: Benjamin Ward, Michael Lomax, Frederic Ransom, and Willie Vann. This installation and the initiation of the first Morehouse students into Delta Chapter were historic events, which were the culmination of a journey that really began in the basement of a church in Augusta, Georgia, where the college was founded not long after the Civil War. Each triennium, we had sent our credentials, and after each rejection, we worked harder for the academic excellence that would qualify us. Now the dream had come true.

If Morehouse has done "so much with so little and so few," it is because many factors converged to make that possible. Good students have been graduated and have acquitted themselves like men after leaving the college. The alumni have made noteworthy contributions to society. The faculty has been able and dedicated. Individual persons and foundations have given the money, without which the College could not have survived. The trustees have been loyal. They always gave me the freedom to do my work, with no restrictions, on the platform or in writing. I was never uneasy about my job, even when I was maliciously and falsely accused of being a Communist or fellow-traveler. In my twenty-seven years as president, I never ceased to raise my voice and pen against the injustices of a society that segregated and discriminated against people because God made them black. No trustee ever took me to task for what I said in public and wrote in books and articles. This may be hard for some people to believe, but it is a fact. Without this kind of confidence and freedom, I would not have remained at Morehouse all those years, particularly since I had seventeen opportunities to leave during that time. I pay high tribute to the men and women who served on the Morehouse Board of Trustees between 1940 and 1967.

I am equally grateful to the persons and foundations that contributed to the college during the years of my presidency. No grant ever came to Morehouse with strings attached. Of course, integrity demands that money be used for the purpose for which it is appropriated, such as for buildings, scholarships, endowments, and other projects. But never was any money given to Morehouse designed to silence my freedom of speech, as I lashed out from time to time against social injustices. A few persons on my faculty never quite believed in my complete freedom from pressure, yet I say emphatically that I state the complete truth. After twenty-seven years, I salute the members of the Board of Trustees, the individual persons and the foundations that assisted Morehouse without trying to tell the College what to do.

It must be said that Charles Merrill did more to vitalize Morehouse than any other individual during my tenure. No one else was more interested in the total program of the College. After the Early-Admissions Program was discontinued by the Ford Foundation, which had sponsored it for eight years, it was Charles Merrill who took up the tab; and he has sponsored the program for more than a decade. During his sponsorship up through 1967, a total of 194 Merrill scholars had entered Morehouse on $500-each scholarships. Thanks to Charles Merrill, sixty Morehouse students have studied and traveled in Europe for a year. At the end of my presidency that year, he had financed travel in Europe for fifty-two faculty members, including their wives or husbands. For many years, Mr. Merrill has been making annual contributions toward faculty salaries. On an annual basis, this one trustee has contributed approximately $75,000 a year for a decade and a half toward the various programs of the College. It is my considered judgment that without Charles Merrill's valiant support, Morehouse would not have been able to qualify for membership in Phi Beta Kappa.

There are many headaches and heartbreaks in raising money. Once in a while, I was made to feel like a dunce when I tried to get money from certain people and foundations for Morehouse. Some with whom I came in contact made me feel very bad. Had it not been for the fact that I loved Morehouse dearly and knew that the cause was worthy, I would have thrown in the sponge. Fairly often, however, I was able to secure money. My heart was made glad when one morning I received an unexpected, long-distance telephone call from Maxwell Hahn of the Field Foundation, informing me that the Foundation had appropriated a half million dollars to Morehouse. Moreover, I made good friends through those twenty-seven years of fund raising. I learned that, on the whole, people with money are fine, generous, human, and understanding. Not all the wealthy can be so characterized, of course, but enough are well-meaning to make me respect and appreciate the rich and those who handle money for them. Among my best friends are persons whom I met when I was trying to raise money for Morehouse.

I shall always cherish the opportunity and the honor that came to me when I was invited to serve a term on the Board of Trustees of the Danforth Foundation, an invitation crowning a friendship with Mr. William H. Danforth, which began in 1942, when I attended my first Associate Conference at Camp Miniwanca.

Largely as a result of this friendship, Mrs. Dorothy Compton (daughter of Mr. Danforth) accepted our invitation to serve as a member of the Morehouse Board of Trustees. Upon her retirement from the Morehouse Board, John Danforth (grandson of William H. Danforth and formerly the Attorney General of the State of Missouri), now senator from the State, joined the Morehouse Board. I appreciated being on the board of the foundation, for few Negroes ever have the opportunity to sit on a board where policies concerning them are determined. A foundation's educational policies involving Negroes are usually made in the absence of Negroes. In 1979, the Ford Foundation elected a Negro, Franklin Thomas, as its president. The Danforth Foundation gave several hundred thousand dollars to Morehouse, and my friendship with the Danforths grew and has been greatly enriched through the years.

I am grateful to the Danforth Foundation and to the Ford Foundation for what they gave to Morehouse. I am similarly grateful to the Rockefeller Foundation, to the Sloan Foundation, to the Woodruff Foundation, the Field Foundation, and many others. To all of these loyal friends of Morehouse, I am glad to pay my vows. They, too, are in the procession of those that have driven me on.

A Summation

I am an old man now, eighty-five years old. I can go back in memory to the end of the last century and can evaluate my experiences beginning in 1898, when I saw my first lynch mob. I can look back eighty years, and I can look forward to the next few years that God may pemit me to live. I hope I can complete two or three more books that continue to haunt my mind.

As I look back there are two contradictory themes in my life. Life has been brutal and cruel to me. Mean, heartbreaking things have crossed my path, and certainly my environment has tried to beat me down and make me accept the philosophy that I had no mission in this world, no call from God to do His will. The path has been so crooked, the road so rocky, the climb so steep, that looking back frightens me even today, and I wonder if I really have made it through to see the innumerable changes that have come about since I was a boy. On the other hand, life has been kind to me; the people have been good to me, black and white. God has been gracious unto me, for I am sure that many good things have come my way by the grace of God, and I have gotten some things that I did not deserve. All during my life, I have done things without ever thinking about being rewarded for what I did, without asking, Will the people applaud me? I have done them because the exigencies of the times required that I do them, and I admit that I have always wanted to do my best, whatever the task or the assignment.

I am inherently competitive. I have always wanted to excel. I have striven to be first, not second, not third. If I wasn't first, it was not because I did not try to be first. If I was beaten, I was a good sport. I had done the best I could, under the circumstances. I was born with a determined will. If denied the thing I sought, I would try again, go to the next person and the next, until I was assured that my wish could not be attained.

I feel that my life has not been lived in vain. I have spoken to thousands of civic, church, fraternal, college, and university congregations throughout North America, Africa, and Asia. I travel across this nation each year, from Boston to California and from Seattle to Maine. I meet people who tell me that my life has meant much to them. These are not Morehouse men alone who graduated from the college during my twenty-seven years as their president, but people who did not attend Morehouse. They are people who have heard me speak and who stop me after a speech, at social gatherings, when introducing me, as they meet me in airports and tell me what I have done for them and thank me for living, for helping them on their way. These are thrilling experiences. Since they are so widespread, I must conclude that my life has meant much to thousands of people. My most precious investment, therefore, has been in people. I have raised millions of dollars for endowment, buildings, and programs, but my life has been invested in people and in my contributions to the church, the college, and the university, to provide scholarships for young people, to help them up the educational ladder. I have spent forty-eight of my years in Atlanta, and I feel that I have helped to make Atlanta a great city, and have earned the respect of its citizens.

Frequently, students ask me what I would do differently if I had to live my life over again. What would I change if I had the power to make changes?

My answer to their question is in two parts. The first part has to do with what I could have done and didn't; this is a sin of omission for which I have asked God to forgive me. My mother and father never went to school a day in their lives. Mother could neither read nor write. Father could read printing, but not script. It was within my power to teach Mother to read and write, and Father to read printing better and to write. These are things I could have done and did not do. Even if God has forgiven me for this sin of omission, the consequences of my neglect can never be erased. The second part of the answer lies in the areas over which I had no control. I could not have changed them. I could do nothing about my school, which ran four months out of the year while the school for whites ran six; nothing about the environment that was designed to beat me and my people down and make us accept in our minds the fallacious doctrine that black people were inherently inferior to whites. I could not do anything about lynchings, segregation, and denigration of black people that infested the South in my time. I did the only things that I could do—get out of Greenwood County, South Carolina; work hard; and pray to God to guide me through the weary years that spread out before me.

There is another answer to the question, "What would I do if I had the option to live my life over again?" With the reservations listed above, I would indeed follow the same programs I have followed since the turn of the century: education, religion, and racial relations. I have always believed that education is imperative for the black man, and his only way out of bondage is to develop his mind so that he will be able to hold his own in a competitive society. I would hold to religion, because without religion and a firm belief and faith in God, the black slaves would hardly have survived. I would strive for better racial relations, because the black man and the white man are both citizens of the United States. Both have fought in every war since the founding of the Republic. Their bodies lie buried in the soil on five or six continents. It would be nonsense for black people and white people to kill each other. No war in the history of man has proved to be necessary! It is my belief that, in time, the slaves would have been freed, thus eliminating the need for the Civil War.

Sadie and I, by choice, elected to spend all of our years in the South against the pull of better-paying jobs in the North and in Switzerland. We never believed that the South could keep the black man down forever. To us, it would have seemed cowardly to leave the South, seeking more and larger freedom for ourselves, leaving our black brothers and sisters here to fight the battle without us. We wanted to be a part of the New South and to fight nonviolently to bring this New South into being. In the fight, we never kowtowed and cringed, never compromised our principles in the fight for justice for all of God's people. I was threatened by the mob three times for riding in Pullman as an interstate passenger. We accepted only the segregation that we had to accept. We never patronized segregated theaters. We drilled it into Morehouse men that they should accept only the segregation that they had to accept.

Jesse O. Thomas, regional secretary of the Southern Urban League in the 20's and 30's, saved Sadie and me from being fired, because, in our two years in Tampa, Florida (1926–1928), during my employment by the league, we insisted that the employment secretary and my wife, Sadie, should be called Miss and Mrs., not because they were black, but because they were women and because that is what white women were called. We were ardent members of the NAACP. Our support for the NAACP is known by three life membership plaques that hang on my walls in my residence and the wall in the New York headquarters of the

NAACP. We supported the NAACP when it was suing to equalize salaries for black teachers and to break down segregation in Southern universities. Sadie and I were a part of the civil-rights struggle from its beginning in early 1960. We supported Martin Luther King, Jr., in his leadership; I participated in the march on Washington in 1963, and would have been in the march from Selma to Montgomery, except that Sadie was very ill at Mayo Clinic at the time, and I had to be there with her. I was tempted again and again to join Martin in the civil-rights movement, but I could not join him without resigning from Morehouse College. My work at Morehouse was not finished.

Emotionally, it was difficult not to join Martin, for he was one of my most beloved students. Friendship began when Martin Luther entered Morehouse College at fourteen. He referred to me as his spiritual mentor. It was my intention to recommend Martin to be my successor at Morehouse, but I am glad now that he accepted the leadership of the nonviolent campaign to free Negroes from servitude. He led the campaign in Montgomery and for one year brought reporters from across the world to see a black leading his people to freedom. As I said in my eulogy at the funeral services of Martin Luther King, Jr., in *Born to Rebel*:

Surely this man was called of God to do this work. If Amos and Micah were prophets in the eighth century, B.C., Martin Luther King, Jr., was a prophet in the twentieth century. If Isaiah was called of God to prophesy in his day, Martin Luther was called of God to prophesy in his time. If Hosea was sent to preach love and forgiveness centuries ago, Martin Luther was sent to expound the doctrine of nonviolence and forgiveness in the third quarter of the twentieth century. If Jesus was sent to release those in prison, was called to preach the gospel to the poor, Martin Luther King, Jr., fits that designation. If a prophet is one who does not seek popular causes to espouse, but rather the causes he thinks are right, Martin Luther qualified on that score.

No! He was not ahead of his time. No man is ahead of his time. Every man is within his star, each in his time. Each man must respond to the call of God in his lifetime and not in somebody else's time. Jesus had to respond to the call of God in the first century, A.D., and not in the twentieth century. He had but one life to live. He couldn't wait. How long do you think Jesus would have had to wait for the constituted authorities to accept him? Twenty-five years? A hundred years? A thousand? He died at thirty-three. He couldn't wait. Paul, Galileo, Copernicus, Martin Luther, the Protestant reformer, Gandhi, and Nehru couldn't wait for another time. They had to act in their lifetimes. No man is ahead of his time. Abraham, leaving the country in obedience to God's call; Moses, leading a rebellious people to the Promised Land; Jesus, dying on a cross; Galileo, on his knees recanting; Lincoln, dying of an assassin's bullet; Woodrow Wilson, crusading for a League of Nations; Martin Luther King, Jr., dying fighting for justice for garbage collectors—none of these men were ahead of their time. With them the time was always ripe to do that which was right and that which needed to be done.

Too bad, you say, that Martin Luther King, Jr., died so young. I feel that way, too. But, as I have said many times before, it isn't how long one lives, but how well. It's what one accomplishes for mankind that matters. Jesus died at thirty-three; Joan of Arc, at nineteen; Byron and Burns, at thirty-six; Keats, at twenty-six; Marlowe, at twenty-nine; Shelley, at thirty; Dunbar, before thirty-five; John Fitzgerald Kennedy, at forty-six; William Rainey Harper, at forty-nine; and Martin Luther King, Jr., at thirty-nine.

We all pray that the assassin will be apprehended and brought to justice. But, make no mistake, the American people are in part responsible for Martin Luther King, Jr.'s death. The assassin heard enough condemnation of King and of Negroes to feel that he had public support. He knew that millions hated King.

The Memphis officials must bear some of the guilt for Martin Luther's assassination. The strike should have been settled several weeks ago. The lowest-paid men in our society should not have to strike for a more just wage. A century after Emancipation, and after the enactment of the 13th, 14th, and 15th Amendments, it should not have been necessary for Martin Luther King, Jr., to stage marches in Montgomery, Birmingham, and Selma, and to go to jail thirty times trying to achieve for his people those rights which people of lighter hue get by virtue of their being born white. We, too, are guilty of murder. It is time for the American people to repent and make democracy equally applicable to all Americans. What can we do? We, not the assassin, represent America at its best. *We* have the power—not the prejudiced, not the assassin—to make things right.

If we love Martin Luther King, Jr., and respect him, as this crowd surely testifies, let us see to it that he did not die in vain; let us see to it that we do not dishonor his name by trying to solve our problems through rioting in the streets. Violence was foreign to his nature. He warned that continued riots could produce a Fascist state. But let us see to it also that the conditions that cause riots are promptly removed, as the President of the United States is trying to get us to do. Let black and white alike search their hearts; and if there be prejudice in our hearts against any racial or ethnic group, let us exterminate it and let us pray, as Martin Luther King, Jr., would pray if he could: *Father, forgive them for they know not what they do.* If we do this, Martin Luther King, Jr., will have died a redemptive death from which all mankind will benefit . . .

I close by saying to you what Martin Luther King, Jr., believed: *If physical death was the price he had to pay to rid America of prejudice and injustice, nothing could be more redemptive.* And to paraphrase the words of the immortal John Fitzgerald Kennedy, Martin Luther King, Jr.'s unfinished work on earth must truly be our own.

I am glad that I did what I did; I have lived to see the New South progress far better than the rest of the country. I believe Atlanta has one of the best black-and-white relationships among the large cities in the United States. Negroes are largely responsible for this. When the South saw that the die had been cast, it accepted the change with grace, and the whites would not now have it otherwise. Negroes are free and white folks are free, and neither would go back to the old days. Particularly, economically and racially, we are better off. I can now sing "Dixie."

The people of the New South have driven me on. Yes, Lord, the people have driven me on; and I thank Thee, God, for these people. It may well be that God had a purpose for the Old South, where the black man's humanity was denied, where all the laws of city, county, state, and federal government were employed to keep Negroes down. It may be that this New South was called to lead Americans to an understanding of what true democracy is.

I am glad that Sadie and I did what we did. I say "we" because we were a team. In forty-three years, our lives were interwoven, interlaced, and intertwined together. Though a trained social worker holding a degree from the University of Chicago School of Social Services, my career was her career. Without Sadie's cooperation, I could not have made Morehouse College the great college that it was and is. Wherever my work called me, she never complained and was always supportive. For example, from South Carolina State to Tampa, from Tampa to Atlanta, from Atlanta to Washington, and from Washington back to Atlanta, Sadie was with me, always finding work on her own until my presidency at Morehouse required all of her time as first lady at the college. I never made a significant move without asking Sadie's opinion. As freshman adviser, Sadie and I did it together. And when I was away, she kept me informed of what was going on at the college. She invited our advisees into our home and taught them the way to act and behave in somebody else's home. Even to this day, I meet students who tell me what those informal meetings at the president's residence meant to them.

With God's help and guidance and with the people obligating me more and more to them, I have done what I understood to be God's will for me and will continue to do this until I die. I have never worried about what will happen to me after death. All through life, I have put my trust in the Lord. Surely, I can trust God to take care of my soul after death.

This volume might well have been entitled "I Beat the System." If there is a thread that connects all I have said in this brief book, it is that I would not let my environment destroy me, beat me down, or make me accept what it said: that my family and my people were inferior to the white man. When a man accepts that designation of inferiority of himself, he might as well die. He has nothing to live for. When he denies his inherent worth and denies that he is a person of infinite worth and value, he is dead even if he lives to be four score years and ten, or even a hundred.

Another thing that one will find in this book is that I am a stubborn man. In order to get where I am, I had to disobey my elders and go against what they told me I should do. I disobeyed my father and my mother, who wanted me to teach in the brickhouse school at twenty-five dollars a month for four months or a hundred dollars a year, and my oldest brother's wife who thought I should teach after highschool graduation to take care of my aging parents. I replied by saying that when my parents reached the time they needed me, I would be able to help them. I was prophetic. From 1921 until my parents died in 1938, I supported them, sending them money each month for maintenance and extra spending money. I disobeyed Reverend Marshall, who didn't want me to leave his Association School in McCormick to go to State College in Orangeburg. When I graduated from State, I did not follow the advice of President Wilkinson who wanted me to take my college work at State. I disobeyed President George Rice Hovey who argued against my going to Bates. Though I had an "A" record, he thought the academic pace at Bates would make it difficult for me and also that the weather in Maine would be too cold for a South Carolina boy. His advice was reasonable, but I had to find out for myself. My mind was made up, and my heart was fixed on a New England college.

The Negro college students who worked out of Boston were Southern boys, students mostly from the South. They told me Boston was cold enough; they thought I should not go to Bates. I did almost freeze to death my first Christmas in Lewiston, when it was forty-four below zero! When I arrived in Lewiston in

September of 1917, the United States was at war with Germany. I conferred with President Chase as to whether I should join the Bates R.O.T.C. He advised me to join. I decided at first to join and even went to Lieutenant Black and signed up. I was to report within two or three days. I couldn't sleep for two nights. I wasn't afraid; I was not unpatriotic, but I was twenty-three years old, and I would be twenty-six when I finished Bates if I stayed in college. A few years in the service would only delay my completion of the college education that I desired so much. I finally reported to the lieutenant that I would not join the R.O.T.C. It made Lieutenant Black furious. He snorted, "It is the duty of every able-bodied man to fight."

Whether my decisions were the right ones, I will never know. Because my hard head has brought me reasonable success, I conclude that I would choose the same path again, were I able to relive my days. I am not advising young people to disobey their elders, but I am suggesting that after one considers all advice, one's life is his, to make it worthwhile or to mar it, to live with honor or die in disgrace. From these two choices, one cannot escape. A person must make his life worthwhile or ruin it.

All during my early years, until I was twenty-six, I had been skating on thin ice, taking risks, taking chances, never knowing how things would turn out. Throughout my early life, I disobeyed my elders. It was risky not to join the R.O.T.C. at Bates. Many faculty people didn't like my decision. It probably was unwise to lead the Pullman porters to send our time slips to Chicago and was partly responsible for my being fired from the Pullman Company. It was a terribly risky thing to cheat my way to Chicago. If the conductor had caught me hiding in a linen closet to get to the university and had put me off the train, would I have ever gotten to the University of Chicago? Only God can answer that question. These are chances I had to take. I took them and won. God must have been with me.

Another person must be mentioned in this book, Lucille Jewel, who was director of the Young Men's and Young Women's Christian Association activities on the campus of South Carolina State College. It was Mrs. Jewel's idea that instead of having a different speaker every Easter, the association should invite one speaker and make the Easter services a statewide activity. She suggested that I be that person. So, beginning in 1936, I gave the Easter message for thirty-one consecutive Easters. They came from all over the state to hear my sermons. White Hall was packed. Loudspeakers were placed outside the assembly hall, and chairs on the lawn. No special merit of mine prompted Mrs. Jewel to do this. Therefore, Lucille must be listed among those to whom I am obligated and among the people who have driven me on.

In concluding this book, *Lord, The People Have Driven Me On,* I feel compelled to bring the readers up to date, giving in brief compass my ten years as President of the Atlanta Board of Education, having been elected to a four-year term three times. I did not want to run and resisted it for a reasonable length of time. Two committees, one black and one white, interviewing me separately, urged me to run for election to the School Board. Finally, I consented. Sadie, my second wife, did not want me to run. She died before the campaign was over. Friends spoke on my behalf while I was visiting the hospital, night and day. They spoke mostly of my record of service at Morehouse and on what I had done for the City of Atlanta. It was thought by some that I would be easy to beat because of my age and because I was a retiree.

Two persons ran against me, one black and the

other one white. At that time, the Board members ran by districts but the entire city voted for him or her. It was rumored around that the white candidate was asked to run because it was believed that I was a bit radical. I beat both opponents, getting more votes than the two combined. During my second campaign, I had only one opponent. She had two emphases: first, she was a retiree from the School System and knew the System; and second, I was too old. It turned out to be no contest. I won overwhelmingly. During the third campaign, the Charter called for six Board members to be elected by districts and three, at-large. A young man, about 25, teaching in the School System came to my office telling me I was too old and suggesting that I step down and support him. I declined his suggestion. Another friend ran at-large against me, but I received approximately 70 percent of the votes cast.

These victories told me something. It said to me that I have made an impact on Atlanta and that the vast majority of the people trust me; with such a display of trust, one cannot let the people down. For eleven years, my eight colleagues on the Board have elected me to serve as their President, testifying that they, too, trust me and respect my leadership. How can I let them down? My Board members are a part of that aggregation that have driven me on. "Yes, Lord, the people have driven me on." We have been sued by the NAACP Legal and Educational Fund. And up to now, we as a Board have held together, not feuding and fussing but discussing and reasoning things out until we reach a conclusion on the issues under discussion. The Board members are biracial. We are friends. We speak to each other. We socialize together. We could not do these things without the Board and Alonzo Crim, the City Superintendent of Schools, working together. Without a doubt, he is one of the ablest superintendents in the United States. I have been swept along and caught up in all these forces, and they are still driving me on.

The Board works by committees. Seven of the Board members are Chairmen and Chairwomen of committees. The Board President and Vice-President, June Cofer, are ex-officio members of all seven committees with voting rights. The committees meet once each month and all members are invited to all committee meetings. The attendance is good, ranging from five to nine present. The Chairperson gives the committee's report and recommends what the Superintendent is to recommend at the official business meetings. All meetings are open to the public and the press, except when the occasion requires privacy. The Board members work like professionals, giving full time. They are able and know the schools located in their areas. The Board members, the Superintendent and his cabinet, the Area Superintendents, Principals, Counselors, and parents are working to give the children of Atlanta the best education attainable. These responsibilities we take seriously and are driven on as if the call came from God.